Good Housekeeping

ESSENTIAL
FREEZE-AHEAD
HANDBOOK

Good Housekeeping
ESSENTIAL
FREEZE-AHEAD
HANDBOOK

All you need to know to make the most of your freezer,
with over 100 recipes

EBURY PRESS
LONDON

First published in 1997

1 3 5 7 9 10 8 6 4 2

First published in the United Kingdom in 1997 by Ebury Press
Random House, 20 Vauxhall Bridge Road, London SW1V 2SA

Random House Australia (Pty) Limited
20 Alfred Street, Milsons Point, Sydney,
New South Wales 2061, Australia

Random House New Zealand Limited
18 Poland Road, Glenfield, Auckland 10, New Zealand

Random House South Africa (Pty) Limited
Endulini, 5a Jubilee Road, Parktown 2193, South Africa

Random House UK Limited Reg. No. 954009

A CIP catalogue record for this book is available from the
British Library.

ISBN 0 09 185209 9

Editor: Julia Canning
Designer: Paul Wood
Introductory text and new recipes: Maxine Clark

Printed and bound in the UK by BPC Hazells, Aylesbury

Contents

Introduction

The freezer is one of the most convenient and useful pieces of kitchen equipment, ideal for preserving and storing perishable foods for long periods. A well-filled freezer means interesting, healthy meals can be prepared quickly with the minimum of effort. This is a great bonus for a wide range of people, from those cooking for a family to a single person who requires fast, easy but delicious food.

THE ADVANTAGES OF FREEZING

- An easy way of keeping food for long periods without deterioration.

- Money can be saved by freezing special offers, economy packs and bulk buys. Cooking in bulk for the freezer is also a good way of making the most of special offers in the shops.

- You can cook when you have the time, and then freeze the results.

- Individual or double portions, or large quantities, can be frozen to suit your needs.

- An overflow of home-grown produce and hedgerow plunder can be frozen to enjoy at a later date.

- Leftovers can be frozen for another day.

- Seasonal produce can be frozen, allowing you to serve them out of season.

CHOOSING A FREEZER

There are two main types – upright and chest freezers – as well as the fridge/freezer. Choose the type to suit the situation and available space. Built-in freezers can be fitted with a matching door. All freezers run off a 13-amp socket outlet and need no special installation.

Upright freezers

These vary in size from small table-top models to full kitchen unit height appliances. The food is stacked on the shelves and in pull-out drawers or baskets, giving easily accessible storage. The shelving suits regular-shaped packets rather than bulky items. Upright freezers are designed to complement refrigerators and normally have reversible doors to match.

Points to consider:

● The drawers should be either plastic-coated wire or solid plastic with solid fronts. Look for easy-grip handles with easy-glide drawers – remember, the drawers will be heavy when filled.
● Drawer stops, which prevent drawers from tipping out when opened, are a useful feature.
● On the whole, drawers are easier to organise than shelves.
● A useful extra feature is a twist-and-serve ice-maker. Once the cubes are made, they can be stored in a box or bag.

Chest freezers

These have a top-opening lid and, because they take up a lot of space, are more suitable for somewhere like a garage than a kitchen. Finding items in a chest freezer can be difficult when the top becomes cluttered. However, chest freezers usually have a larger capacity than the largest uprights, so if you want to store a large quantity of food and have the space, a chest freezer could be the right choice.

Fridge/freezers

As a general rule, the freezer is usually under the refrigerator compartment. Capacities vary – the freezer and refrigerator may be equal in size, or one compartment may be larger than the other. Some American-style units are arranged side-by-side and have extra features.

Look for compartments with separate controls, so that the freezer can be switched off independently for defrosting manually, and the refrigerator switched off when you go away.

Defrosting systems

FROST-FREE UPRIGHT FREEZERS: These larger capacity freezers do not need to be defrosted as there is no build-up of frost. The lack of water vapour prevents the build-up, ensuring that the freezer runs at maximum efficiency and returns to the right temperature more quickly when the door is opened. With the frost-free system the drawers run smoothly, the labels remain clear and food does not stick together. However, frost-free freezers tend to be more expensive to buy and run.

LOW-FROST CHEST FREEZERS: Ordinary chest freezers need defrosting once a year, but low-frost freezers are 80% more efficient and only need defrosting every five years or so. The low-frost system prevents an intake of moisture, except for the moisture which enters when the lid is opened, creating frost. Running costs are reduced with this system.

HOW FREEZING WORKS

'Frozen food' is food that has been fast-frozen to a temperature of 18°C (0°F). The fast-freezing process forms ice crystals which are small enough not to damage unduly the structure of the food. This means that when the food is thawed and cooked it does not lose too much moisture. The freezing process also immobilises (but does not kill) any bacteria which can spoil the food.

FREEZER SAFETY

As soon as frozen food is thawed it should be consumed, otherwise it will become unsafe to eat.

● Never switch the freezer off, except when defrosting, otherwise you may lose the entire contents of your freezer.

● It is a good idea to tape the switch to the 'on' position if it is in a run of sockets, or to colour code your plugs.

● If you have small children, buy a model which has controls they cannot reach.

EMERGENCIES

In the case of a power cut or when the machine is accidentally switched off DO NOT PANIC. Frozen foods take a long time to thaw and will be fine for a few hours.

● If you have advance warning of a power cut, turn on the fast-freeze switch or turn the control to maximum, making sure that the freezer is full – use old towels or newspapers to fill spaces.

● Cover with a blanket or rug to insulate, but leave the condenser and pipes free.

● Do not open the door until several hours after the appliance has started to work again.

● If it is only your freezer that is affected, try to store the contents in a friend's freezer!

● Food in a chest freezer will be safe for about 48 hours without power. Food in an upright freezer will keep for about 30 hours.

● If all else fails, cook raw items to freeze again. Cook and consume as much as possible. Throw away anything that you think might be unsafe, to avoid the risk of food poisoning – it is not worth the small saving!

● Take out freezer insurance, which is usually available on a house contents policy. Check how much you are covered for. Keep an itemised list of the contents for the inspector.

FREEZER PACKAGING

For some frozen foods you will need special packaging; others can be stored in existing items from your kitchen, such as plastic storage boxes and casseroles.

POLYTHENE BAGS: Choose a heavy gauge, recommended for freezing. Seal with twist ties or use plastic clips specially made for the purpose. A heat-sealing device can also be used. Some bags are colour-coded, which makes identification easier.

FREEZER FILM: This must be used to cover and wrap acidic foods that may react with foil. Overwrap with foil after covering closely. Do not use ordinary cling film.

FOIL: Choose special, thick freezer foil to use in a single layer; alternatively, use a double layer of ordinary foil. Do not wrap acidic foods directly in foil.

INTERLEAVING: Greaseproof or polythene sheets, foil or freezer film are used to separate items of food which may stick together when packed – eg pancakes, fish fillets, steaks, sausages.

CONTAINERS: Use foil, plastic, ceramic, Pyrex or any other freezerproof container. Square shapes pack better than round.

FREEZER TAPE: To avoid the frustration of tape that doesn't stick properly, buy freezer tape, which is made for use in low temperatures!

LABELS: Don't be tempted not to label – it's difficult to identify food once it's frozen. Choose special freezer labels that will stick; brightly coloured ones are particularly good. Write on the contents, weight and date. Use a freezer pen – it will be waterproof! If you are really organised, include cooking instructions.

OVERWRAPPING: Ideally, overwrap any commercial product in foil or film to keep in peak condition. Overwrap anything that looks as if it might come undone in the freezer. If only using a few pieces of product at a time, remember to exclude the air before re-wrapping.

FREEZING TECHNIQUES

● Use only top-quality food, and handle it as little as possible.

● If the food is already frozen, get it home and into the freezer as fast as possible – keep a cheap insulated bag in the car for this purpose.

● Freeze in small quantities – food will freeze faster and take less time to thaw.

● Wrap and pack solid food carefully to exclude air and moisture, both of which can damage food. You can buy a vacuum pump to help remove air.

● When freezing liquids, leave room for expansion – a lid will be pushed off if the container is overfilled.

● Always chill cooked food in the refrigerator before freezing. NEVER put anything warm or hot in the freezer – the resulting rise in temperature will damage food already in the freezer.

● Label, colour-code and date food clearly and, if possible, keep a log book so that you can rotate food easily.

● Never freeze more than one-tenth of your freezer's capacity in any 24 hours, as this can badly affect the temperature.

● Allocate certain areas in the freezer for different types of food, eg raw meat, raw fish, prepared dishes.

FAST-FREEZE SWITCH Use this when adding food to the freezer, unless it is a very small quantity, such as a loaf of bread.

SAFE THAWING

THESE GUIDELINES ARE VERY IMPORTANT:

● Cover food loosely while thawing.

● Always thaw at cool room temperature, ie in a larder or in the refrigerator. A warm environment will encourage the growth of bacteria.

● Make sure that food thawed in the refrigerator is completely defrosted before cooking, to prevent the risk of food poisoning. There should be absolutely no ice crystals in evidence, especially when dealing with poultry and joints of meat, otherwise the internal cooking temperature may not be hot enough to destroy any dangerous bacteria in the meat. Poultry must feel supple, the legs loose and the cavity free from ice crystals.

● Always allow more than enough time to thaw, especially with large birds such as turkeys.

● Cook food as soon as possible after thawing.

● Always drain off and throw away any liquid lost during thawing, and do not allow it to touch any other food. A defrosting tray is useful – this has a drip tray which catches the liquid lost during thawing, keeping the liquid separate from the thawed food.

THAWING IN A MICROWAVE: A microwave is useful for cutting down the thawing time of certain foods; some models will do this automatically. They are particularly useful for thawing and reheating prepared meals. Always follow the instructions in the manual or on the inside of the packet.

WATCHPOINTS:

● Never re-freeze anything that has accidentally thawed over a few days.

● Never re-freeze thawed food unless you have cooked it again. For example, thawed raw mince can be cooked into a bolognese sauce and then frozen. But thawed raw mince cannot be re-frozen in its raw state.

(Note that thawed raw shellfish should never be re-frozen either raw or in cooked form.)

● Do not re-freeze ice cream, raw pastry or uncooked baked goods once thawed.

USEFUL TIPS

FREEZING CASSEROLES: To freeze the contents of a casserole, line a dish with foil or a bag, pour in the food, remove air, seal and freeze. When frozen, pull the frozen pack out of the dish, label and return to freezer.

FREEZING BREAD: Frozen sliced bread is always useful – simply pop a frozen slice directly into the toaster for a little longer than normal.

FREEZING HERBS: Place chopped fresh herbs in ice-cube trays and top up with water. Freeze, then store in plastic boxes. Particularly good for garnishing chilled soups just before serving.

FREEZING STOCK: Frozen stock is always handy – freeze concentrated stock in ice-cube trays, store in plastic boxes and simply add directly to pan of ingredients.

Quick Guide to Freezer Storage Times

DAIRY PRODUCE

cream	6-8 months
butter (unsalted)	6-8 months
butter (salted)	3-4 months
cheese (hard)	4-6 months
cheese (soft)	3-4 months
ice cream, mousses etc	3-4 months

FISH

white fish	6-8 months
oily fish	3-4 months
fish portions	3-4 months
shellfish	2-3 months

FRUIT AND VEGETABLES

fruit in syrup	9-12 months
fruit (without added sugar)	6-8 months
fruit purée	6-8 months
fruit juice	4-6 months
vegetables	
(blanched – most varieties)	10-12 months

MEAT AND POULTRY

beef and lamb	4-6 months
pork and veal	4-6 months
offal	2 months
sliced bacon and cured meat	2-3 months
bacon and ham joints	3-4 months
chicken and turkey	4-6 months
duck and goose	4-6 months
venison	4-6 months
rabbit, hare and game	4-6 months
sausages and sausagemeat	2-3 months
minced red meat	3-4 months

PREPARED FOODS

bread and bread rolls	2-3 months
other yeast products and pastries	3-4 months
cakes	4-6 months
sandwiches	2-3 months
soups and sauces	3 months
ready meals	4-6 months
if highly seasoned	2-3 months
stock	6 months

FREEZING FRESH VEGETABLES

Freeze only those vegetables that are really fresh – within 12 hours of their being picked. Most vegetables keep better for longer if blanched before freezing.

To blanch vegetables conventionally, immerse up to 450 g (1 lb) at a time in a large pan of boiling water (a preserving pan is good for this). Bring back to the boil (see chart for blanching times). Remove and put straight into a bowl of iced water to cool them. Blanching water can be used 6-7 times and the cooling water can be kept cool by the repeated addition of ice cubes or frozen ice blocks. A blanching basket makes this task easier; otherwise use a large square of muslin or a suitable strainer.

For small quantities, blanching can be done in a microwave. Place the vegetables in a bowl containing 45 ml (3 tbsp) cold water and heat on full power for 3-5 minutes, stirring halfway through. Small diced or sliced vegetables need only a short time; large, dense root vegetables will need longer. Allow standing time of 1 minute before cooling as above and freezing.

Although blanching improves the texture of vegetables that are to be stored for some time, it is not essential to blanch those which will be eaten within a few weeks.

VEGETABLE	PREPARATION	BLANCHING TIME
Artichokes, globe	Wash in cold water, add a little lemon juice to the blanching water, blanch, cool, and drain upside-down on kitchen paper. Pack in rigid containers.	4-5 minutes
Asparagus	Grade into thick and thin stems but don't tie into bunches. Wash in cold water, blanch, cool and drain. Tie into small bundles.	Thin – 1 minute Thick –2 minutes
Aubergines	Peel and cut roughly into 2.5 cm (1 inch) slices. Blanch, cool and dry on kitchen paper. Pack in layers in rigid containers, separated by interleaving paper.	1-2 minutes
Beans, French, runner, broad	French: trim ends and blanch. Runner: slice thickly and blanch. Broad: shell and blanch. In each case, cool, drain and pack.	1 minute 1 minute 1½ minutes
Beetroot	Choose small beetroot up to 5 cm (2 inches) in diameter. Wash well and rub skin off after blanching. Beetroot under 2.5 cm (1 inch) in diameter may be frozen whole; others should be sliced or diced. Pack in rigid containers. NOTE: Long storage can make beetroot rubbery.	Small whole – 5 minutes Large – cook until tender
Broccoli	Wash in salted water and cut into small sprigs. Blanch, cool and drain. Pack in boxes in 1-2 layers, tips to stalks.	1 minute
Brussels sprouts	Trim, removing discoloured outer leaves. Blanch, cool and drain.	½-1 minute
Carrots	If left whole, scrape after blanching. Slice or cut into small dice. Blanch, cool, drain and pack.	2-3 minutes
Cauliflower	Break into small florets about 5 cm (2 inches) in diameter. Add the juice of a lemon to the blanching water to keep them white; blanch, cool, drain and pack.	1 minute
Celeriac	Cook until almost tender, peel and slice. Cool, then pack.	
Celery	Cut into 2.5 cm (1 inch) lengths. Use for cooked dishes.	
Chillies	Remove stalks and scoop out the seeds and pithy part. Blanch, cool, drain and pack.	10 seconds

Corn on the cob	Select young yellow kernels, not starchy, over-ripe or shrunken. Remove husks and 'silks'. Blanch, cool and dry. Pack individually in freezer polythene or foil. NOTE: Freezing may cause loss of flavour and tenderness.	Small – 2 minutes Medium – 3 minutes Large – 4 minutes
Courgettes	Wash and cut into 1 cm (½ inch) slices. Blanch, cool, drain and pack.	10 seconds
Fennel	Trim and slice thinly. Blanch, cool, drain and pack.	30 seconds
Kohlrabi	Choose small roots, 5-7 cm (2-3 inches) in diameter. Cut off tops, peel and dice. Blanch, cool, drain and pack.	1 minute
Leeks	Cut into 1 cm (½ inch) slices and wash well. Blanch, cool, drain, pack and freeze. Only suitable for casseroles or soups.	30 seconds
Mangetout	Trim the ends. Blanch, cool, drain and pack.	10 seconds
Marrow	Choose young marrows. Peel, cut into 1-2.5 cm (½-1 inch) slices, blanch, cool, drain and pack.	10 seconds
Onions	Peel, finely chop, blanch and pack in small rigid containers for cooking later; packages should be overwrapped to prevent the smell filtering out. Button onions may be blanched whole and used in casseroles.	1 minute Button onions – 2 minutes
Parsnips	Choose young parsnips, trim, peel and cut into narrow strips. Blanch, cool, drain and pack.	1 minute
Peas, green	Shell and blanch. Shake the blanching basket from time to time to distribute the heat evenly. Cool, drain and pack in polythene bags or rigid containers.	1 minute
Peppers, sweet, green, red, yellow	Wash well, remove stems, seeds and membranes. Blanch as halves or in thin slices. For better colour, if storage is less than 6 months, do not blanch.	1 minute
Potatoes	Best frozen cooked, as in croquettes or gratin dishes.	1 minute
Pumpkins	Peel, remove seeds and membrane, then cut into large dice. Blanch, cool, drain and pack in rigid containers. Or cook and freeze in purée form.	2 minutes
Spinach	Blanch in small quantities, cool quickly and press out excess moisture, or purée. Pack in rigid containers or polythene bags.	10 seconds
Squash	Peel, remove seeds where necessary, and cut into large dice. Blanch, cool, drain and pack in rigid containers.	½-1 minute, depending on type
Tomatoes	Tomatoes are most useful frozen as purée. Small whole ones packed in bags and frozen can be used in cooked dishes. To purée tomatoes, skin, then simmer in their own juice for 5 minutes, until soft. Rub through a nylon sieve or purée in a blender or food processor, cool and pack in small containers.	
Turnips	Trim and peel. Cut into small dice, about 1 cm (½ inch). Blanch, cool, drain and pack in rigid containers.	2½ minutes

FREEZING FRESH FRUIT

Fruit which is to be frozen should be perfectly ripe and free from any blemishes.

Overripe fruit can be frozen in the form of a purée. With fruits such as apples you will have to cook them first before puréeing, but fruits such as peaches can be peeled, stoned and puréed in their fresh form.

When freezing fruit, first consider how you are likely to use it when you come to eat it and prepare accordingly. Small fruits that don't need peeling are best frozen as they are. Remove stalks where appropriate and spread them out either on special open-freezing trays or on baking sheets or trays lined with non-stick greaseproof paper. Once frozen, they can be stored in bags and will not stick to each other, so you can easily remove just the quantity required.

Firm-textured fruits and those which tend to discolour should be frozen in a syrup made up as indicated in the chart. Dissolve the sugar in the water, add lemon juice where indicated and leave to cool before putting in the fruit. Light fruits which tend to float to the surface should be kept below it by putting a damp, crumpled piece of non-absorbent paper on top. Leave 1-2 cm (about ½ inch) headspace for the liquid to expand. Most frozen fruit in syrup will keep for 9-12 months. Open frozen fruit and purées keep for 6-8 months; fruit juices 4-6 months.

FRUIT	PREPARATION
Apples	Use one of the following methods: ● Peel, core and cut into 5 mm (¼ inch) slices. Drop into water with lemon juice added. Blanch for 2-3 minutes and cool in ice-cold water before packing; useful for pies and flans. ● Purée – peel, core and stew the apples in the minimum amount of water – sweetened or unsweetened. Purée or mash. Leave to cool before packing.
Apricots	Plunge into boiling water for 30 seconds to loosen the skins, then peel. Then prepare in one of the following ways: ● Cut in half or slice into cold syrup – 450 g (1 lb) sugar to 1 litre (1¾ pints) water with the juice of a lemon added to prevent browning. Immerse the apricots by placing a piece of clean, crumpled, non-absorbent paper on the fruit, under the lid. ● Leave whole and freeze in syrup. In time, an almond flavour may develop around the stone. ● Purée – cook apricots in very little water with sugar to taste, then purée.
Blackberries	Wash and dry fruit. Open-freeze. Pack in rigid containers.
Blackcurrants	Use one of the following methods: ● Open-freeze whole fruit. ● Purée – cook to a purée with very little water and brown sugar to taste.
Blueberries or Bilberries	Open-freeze whole fruit.
Cherries	Use one of the following methods: ● Open-freeze whole fruit; best used for pie fillings. ● Cover with cold syrup – 450 g (1 lb) sugar to 1 litre (1¾ pints) water; leave headspace. Take care not to open until required, as fruit loses colour rapidly on exposure to the air.
Damsons	The skins are inclined to toughen during freezing. Best packing methods are: ● Purée – cook damsons in very little water with sugar to taste, then rub through a nylon sieve. ● Halve, remove the stones and pack in cold syrup – 450 g (1 lb) sugar to 1 litre (1¾ pints) water; they will need cooking after freezing and can be used as stewed fruit. ● Poach and sweeten.
Figs	Wash the figs gently to avoid bruising. Avoid freezing very ripe figs. Remove stems. Open-freeze, either whole or peeled, then pack in polythene bags.

Gooseberries

Use one of the following methods:
- Open-freeze whole fruit; use for pie fillings.
- Purée – stew fruit in a very little water, rub through a nylon sieve and sweeten.

Grapefruit

Not worth freezing.

Greengages

Halve, remove stones and cover with cold syrup – 450 g (1 lb) sugar to 1 litre (1¾ pints) water, with the juice of 1 lemon added. Pack in rigid containers. Do not open until required as the fruit loses colour. Skins tend to toughen.

Lemons and Limes

Use one of the following methods:
- Open-freeze – whole lemons, slices or segments.
- Juice: Squeeze the juice and freeze in ice-cube trays; transfer frozen cubes to polythene bags for storage.
- Julienne strips: Remove all pith from the peel, cut into thin strips, blanch for 1 minute, cool and pack; use for garnishing dishes.

Loganberries

Remove stalks and open-freeze whole fruit.

Mangoes and Papayas

Peel and slice ripe fruit into cold syrup – 450 g (1 lb) sugar to 1 litre (1¾ pints) water; add 30 ml (2 tbsp) lemon juice to each 1 litre (1¾ pints) syrup.

Oranges

Use one of the following methods:
- Peel, segment and pack in cold syrup – use equal quantities of sugar and water; add any juice from the fruit to the syrup.
- Open-freeze whole fruit – good way of storing Seville oranges to use later for making marmalade.
- Juice: Squeeze the juice, add sugar if desired and freeze in small quantities in containers or in ice-cube trays.
- Julienne strips: Remove all pith from the peel, cut into thin strips, blanch for 1 minute, cool and pack; use for garnishing dishes.

Peaches

Really ripe peaches are best skinned and stoned under running water, as scalding will soften and slightly discolour the flesh. Plunge firm peaches in boiling water for 30 seconds, then skin. Brush with lemon juice. Use one of the following methods:
- Cover halves or slices with cold syrup – 450 g (1 lb) sugar to 1 litre (1¾ pints) water, with the juice of 1 lemon added. Pack in rigid containers, leaving headspace.
- Purée, then mix in 15 ml (1 tbsp) lemon juice and 125 g (4 oz) sugar to each 450 g (1 lb) fruit – suitable for sorbets.

Pineapple

Peel and core, then slice, dice, crush or cut into wedges. Use one of the following methods:
- Pack unsweetened in layers, separated by non-stick paper, in rigid containers.
- Cover with cold syrup – 450 g (1 lb) sugar to 1 litre (1¾ pints) water, including any pineapple juice from the preparation. Pack in rigid containers, leaving headspace.
- Pack crushed pineapple in rigid containers.

Plums

Use one of the following methods:
- Halve and discard stones. Cover in cold syrup – 450 g (1 lb) sugar to 1 litre (1¾ pints) water with the juice of 1 lemon. Pack in rigid containers. Do not open until required, as the fruit loses colour.
- Poach and sweeten.

Redcurrants

Open-freeze whole fruit.

Rhubarb

Trim into 1-2.5 cm (½-1 inch) lengths. Blanch in boiling water for 1 minute and cool quickly. Freeze chopped or pared. Use for pies and crumbles.

Strawberries and Raspberries

Remove stalks, then use one of the following methods:
- Open-freeze whole fruit – suitable for raspberries; strawberries can be a disappointment.
- Purée and sweeten to taste – about 225 g (8 oz) sugar to every 225 g (8 oz) purée; add a little lemon juice to strawberry purée.

SOUPS AND STARTERS

Beetroot and Orange Soup

Beetroot combines perfectly with tangy orange to create a delicious soup, full of sophisticated flavours. Ideal for entertaining, the soup freezes well and can be reheated in a matter of minutes.

Preparation time: 15 minutes
Cooking time: 2 hours 25 minutes
Cals per serving: 230

Serves 6

700 g (1½ lb) medium-sized raw beetroot	**300 ml (½ pint) medium-dry sherry**
225 g (8 oz) onions	**300 ml (½ pint) orange juice**
225 g (8 oz) potatoes	**salt and pepper**
50 g (2 oz) butter	**TO GARNISH**
1.3 litres (2¼ pints) vegetable stock	**pared orange rind strips**

1 Trim the beetroot, then wrap in foil and place in a large roasting tin. Cook at 200°C (400°F) Mark 6 for 1½ hours. Remove from the oven, leave to cool, then peel and roughly chop. Peel and roughly chop the onions and potatoes.

2 Heat the butter in a large, heavy-based saucepan. Add the onions and cook for 10 minutes or until golden and soft. Stir in the beetroot and potatoes and coat with the buttery juices.

3 Add the stock, sherry and orange juice, bring to the boil, then cover and simmer for 40 minutes or until the potatoes are tender.

4 Cool the soup slightly, then purée in batches in a food processor or blender until smooth.

5 Return the soup to the wiped-out pan and adjust the seasoning. Bring back to the boil and serve garnished with orange rind strips.

TO FREEZE: Cool, pack and freeze at the end of step 4.
TO USE: Thaw overnight at cool room temperature. Bring back to the boil, adding stock or water if the soup is too thick. Simmer for 10 minutes and adjust the seasoning. Garnish as above.

Spinach and Blue Cheese Soup

A mouthwatering partnership of fresh spinach and blue cheese, this rich and creamy soup provides a luxurious start to a vegetarian meal – and is surprisingly easy to make.

Preparation time: 25 minutes
Cooking time: 40 minutes
Cals per serving: 560
Serves 6

450 g (1 lb) fresh spinach	**600 ml (1 pint) vegetable stock**
225 g (8 oz) onions	**300 ml (½ pint) double cream**
350 g (12 oz) leeks	**pepper**
350 g (12 oz) blue cheese, such as Stilton, Roquefort or Dolcelatte	**TO GARNISH**
50 g (2 oz) butter	**crisply fried sliced leek**
	crumbled blue cheese

1 Remove the stalks from the spinach and rinse the leaves well in cold, running water. Drain and finely chop. Peel and roughly chop the onions. Trim, clean and roughly chop the leeks. Crumble the cheese.

2 Melt the butter in a large, heavy-based saucepan, add the onions and leeks and cook for 20 minutes or until golden and very soft, stirring occasionally. Add the stock, cream and cheese; bring to the boil. Simmer the soup, uncovered, for 10 minutes. Add the spinach and bring back to the boil. Simmer for 5 minutes.

3 Cool the soup slightly, then purée in batches in a food processor or blender until smooth. Push through a fine sieve.

4 Return the soup to wiped-out pan. Bring to the boil and add pepper to taste. Serve in warm soup bowls, garnished with fried leeks and crumbled blue cheese.

TO FREEZE: Cool, pack and freeze at the end of step 3.
TO USE: Thaw the soup overnight at cool room temperature. Bring to the boil and complete to the end of the recipe.

Minestrone Alla Milanese

Packed with mixed vegetables, this classic Italian soup makes a substantial first course. Served with ciabatta, it is also perfect as a light lunch dish.

Preparation time: 40 minutes
Cooking time: 1 hour 20 minutes
Cals per serving: 345

Serves 6

125 g (4 oz) pancetta or streaky bacon	75 g (3 oz) Savoy cabbage
450 g (1 lb) onions	50 g (2 oz) butter
175 g (6 oz) carrots	1.7 litres (3 pints) beef stock
175 g (6 oz) swede or turnip	400 g (14 oz) can chopped tomatoes
175 g (6 oz) potatoes	salt and pepper
125 g (4 oz) celery	400 g (14 oz) can cannellini or borlotti beans, drained and rinsed
125 g (4 oz) courgettes	
75 g (3 oz) French beans	50 g (2 oz) freshly grated Parmesan cheese

1 Cut the pancetta into small dice. Peel and dice the onions, carrots, swede and potatoes. Trim and dice the celery and courgettes. Finely chop the French beans. Finely shred the cabbage.

2 Melt the butter in a large saucepan. Sauté the pancetta and onions for 5 minutes or until soft, stirring frequently. Stir in the carrots, swede and celery and sauté for 5 minutes.

3 Add the courgettes, French beans and potatoes. Cook, stirring, for about 5 minutes or until all the vegetables are coated in butter.

4 Add the Savoy cabbage with the beef stock and chopped tomatoes. Add salt and pepper to taste. Bring to the boil, then cover and simmer for 45 minutes. Add the beans and cook for a further 15 minutes.

5 Stir in half the Parmesan cheese and serve the soup, with the remaining Parmesan handed round separately.

TO FREEZE: Complete to the end of step 4. Cool, pack and freeze.

TO USE: Thaw overnight at cool room temperature. Bring back to the boil, cover and simmer for 10 minutes. Complete as in step 5.

Bacon and Chestnut Soup

Filled with rich flavours, this elegant chestnut soup is the perfect choice for the festive season. Well suited to freezing, simply reheat it at the last moment and swirl in cream and sherry to serve.

Preparation time: 15 minutes
Cooking time: about 30 minutes
Cals per serving: 280

Serves 4

75 g (3 oz) streaky bacon	**250 g (9 oz) cooked chestnuts, peeled**
50 g (2 oz) celery	**1.4 litres (2½ pints) chicken stock**
125 g (4 oz) onion	**salt and pepper**
50 g (2 oz) carrots	**TO SERVE**
25 g (1 oz) butter	**30 ml (2 tbsp) sherry**
5 ml (1 tsp) dried thyme	**50 ml (2 fl oz) single cream**

1 Roughly chop the bacon and celery. Peel and roughly chop the onion and carrots.

2 Melt the butter in a saucepan and add the bacon, vegetables and the thyme. Cook, stirring, for 7-10 minutes or until slightly softened and golden.

3 Add the chestnuts and stock and season with salt and pepper. Cover and cook for about 20 minutes. Remove from the heat and allow to cool a little. Blend in a food processor or blender until smooth.

4 To serve, reheat gently, add the sherry and the cream and serve.

TO FREEZE: Cool, cover and freeze at the end of step 3.
TO USE: Thaw overnight at cool room temperature and complete as in step 4.

Clear Chicken and Mushroom Soup

If you can find lemon grass in your local supermarket or in Oriental shops, add a stick to the simmering soup in step 2 as it will give it a wonderful lemon fragrance.

Preparation time: 15 minutes
Cooking time: 40 minutes
Cals per serving: 265
Serves 4

175 g (6 oz) onion	**salt and pepper**
25 g (1 oz) piece fresh root ginger	**125 g (4 oz) button mushrooms**
2 chicken legs, about 450 g (1 lb) total weight	**6 spring onions**
30 ml (2 tbsp) oil	**60 ml (4 tbsp) sherry**
50 g (2 oz) long-grain rice	**dash of Worcestershire sauce**
15 ml (1 tbsp) soy sauce	

1 Peel and slice the onions; peel and finely chop the ginger. Skin the chicken legs and halve each portion. Heat the oil in a large saucepan. Add the onion and lightly brown. Stir in the ginger and rice and fry for about 30 seconds.

2 Pour in 1.7 litres (3 pints) water with the soy sauce and bring to the boil. Add the chicken pieces and season with salt and pepper. Cover and simmer for about 30 minutes or until the chicken and rice are tender.

3 Meanwhile, slice the mushrooms; cut the spring onions into fine shreds.

4 Remove the chicken from the pan and shred the flesh. Return to the pan with the mushrooms, spring onions, sherry and Worcestershire sauce. Simmer gently for about 5 minutes then adjust the seasoning to serve.

TO FREEZE: Cool, pack and freeze at the end of step 4.
TO USE: Thaw overnight at cool room temperature, then reheat to serve.

Crab and Tomato Soup

Dressed crabs are available in most supermarkets, with the white and dark meat neatly separated. This recipe uses both meats and the shell!

Preparation time: 40 minutes
Cooking time: 45 minutes
Cals per serving: 270

Serves 6

one dressed crab, about 200 g (7 oz)	**45 ml (3 tbsp) mayonnaise**
125 g (4 oz) onion	**5 ml (1 tsp) tomato ketchup**
1 garlic clove	**Tabasco sauce**
1 celery stick	**Worcestershire sauce**
60 ml (4 tbsp) olive oil	**salt and pepper**
60 ml (4 tbsp) port	**50 g (2 oz) Emmenthal cheese**
1.1 litres (2 pints) vegetable stock	**1 small French stick**
550 g (1¼ lb) tomato passata or creamed tomatoes	**TO GARNISH**
	single cream

1 Separate the white and brown crab meat; set aside. Roughly crush the shell. Peel and chop the onion. Peel and crush the garlic. Trim and chop the celery.

2 Heat 30 ml (2 tbsp) oil in a large saucepan, add the crab shell and the vegetables and cook for 5 minutes, stirring all the time. Add the port and bring to the boil. Bubble until all the liquid has evaporated. Pour in the stock and passata or creamed tomatoes and bring to the boil. Add the brown crab meat, then simmer, covered, for 30 minutes.

3 Strain the crab soup through a sieve, pressing to extract the juices. Discard the shell and vegetables.

4 Wipe out the pan, return the soup and bring back to the boil. Whisk in the mayonnaise, tomato ketchup, garlic, a few drops of Tabasco, Worcestershire sauce and seasoning.

5 Grate the cheese. Thinly slice the bread, then toast on one side under a hot grill. Drizzle the remaining oil over the untoasted side and sprinkle with the grated cheese. Cook under the grill until bubbling.

6 Stir the flaked white crab meat into the soup and heat through for 1-2 minutes. Ladle the hot soup into warmed, ovenproof bowls. Garnish with a swirl of single cream, float the warm croûtes on top and serve immediately.

TO FREEZE: Cool, pack and freeze the soup at the end of step 4.

TO USE: Thaw overnight at cool room temperature, then complete to the end of the recipe.

Chicken Liver and Peppercorn Pâté

A useful pâté to have as a standby in the freezer for last-minute entertaining.

Preparation time: 20 minutes, plus chilling
Cooking time: 15 minutes
Cals per serving: 430 cals
Serves 8

175 g (6 oz) onion	**15-30 ml (1-2 tbsp) lemon juice**
2 garlic cloves	**45 ml (3 tbsp) brandy**
175 g (6 oz) rindless streaky bacon	**30 ml (2 tbsp) green or pink peppercorns in brine**
700 g (1½ lb) chicken livers	**TO GARNISH**
225 g (8 oz) butter	**green peppercorns**
7.5 ml (1½ tsp) dried marjoram	**bay leaves**
salt and pepper	

1 Peel and chop the onion. Peel and crush the garlic. Cut the bacon into small pieces. Rinse and drain the livers, removing any stringy parts, then cut each into three pieces.

2 Heat 75 g (3 oz) butter in a large frying pan. Add the onions and bacon and cook over a moderate heat until they begin to brown, stirring occasionally.

3 Increase the heat, stir in the livers with the garlic, marjoram and salt and pepper. Fry for about 3 minutes, stirring frequently, until all the ingredients are well browned, with the livers still retaining a hint of pink inside. Cool the mixture for about 15 minutes.

4 Transfer the contents of the pan to a food processor and add a further 75 g (3 oz) softened butter, the lemon juice, brandy and the drained peppercorns. Blend until almost smooth. Adjust the seasoning.

5 Turn the mixture into a serving dish – there should be about 1 cm (½ inch) space at the top. Cover the dish and chill for 2 hours or until set.

6 Melt the remaining butter and skim. Arrange the peppercorns and bay leaves on top of the pâté and spoon the butter over. Cover and refrigerate to set. Bring to room temperature before serving.

TO FREEZE: Overwrap and freeze at the end of step 5.
TO USE: Thaw overnight at cool room temperature; finish as in step 6.

Thai Sesame Prawn Toasts

A treat from the Orient, these tasty little toasts, with their crisp prawn and sesame seed topping, make an irresistible starter – and they can be quickly reheated from frozen.

Preparation time: 30 minutes, plus chilling
Cooking time: about 15 minutes
Cals per serving: 246
Serves 10

1 cm (½ inch) piece fresh root ginger	5 ml (1 tsp) salt
1 cm (½ inch) piece lemon grass stalk	30 ml (2 tbsp) finely chopped fresh coriander
1 small red chilli	10-12 slices stale white bread
700 g (1½ lb) fresh raw prawn tails	40 g (1½ oz) sesame seeds
7.5 ml (1½ tsp) cornflour	40 g (1½ oz) black mustard seeds
10 ml (2 tsp) dry sherry	oil for deep-frying
1 egg white, lightly beaten	chilli sauce for dipping

1 Peel and finely chop the ginger; very finely chop the lemon grass; deseed and finely chop the chilli.

2 Peel the prawns. Using a sharp knife, make a slit down the centre of the back and remove the instestinal vein. Rinse under cold running water, drain and pat dry with kitchen paper.

3 Place the prawns in a food processor with the ginger and lemon grass and work to a smooth paste.

4 Mix the cornflour, sherry and egg white together with the salt. With the machine running, gradually add the egg white mixture to the prawns. Do not overprocess. Transfer to a bowl and beat in the chilli and coriander. Cover and chill in the refrigerator for 1 hour until the mixture firms up a little.

5 Cut the crusts off the bread and trim into equal squares. Spread a generous amount of paste on to each slice, mounding the paste slightly in the middle, leaving less at the edge.

6 Mix the sesame and mustard seeds together and dip the prawn-coated side of each piece of bread into the seeds, pressing lightly to coat well.

7 Heat the oil in a deep-fat fryer to 180°C (350°F). Fry the coated bread pieces, two at a time, for about 3 minutes, turning once until light golden brown. (You will hear some of the mustard seeds popping – don't worry!) Remove the toasts and drain on kitchen paper. Cut each toast diagonally into 4 small triangles and serve immediately with a chilli dipping sauce.

TO FREEZE: In step 7, allow the fried toasts to cool completely. Do not cut. Layer with freezerproof film and freeze.

TO USE: Place the frozen toasts on baking sheets and reheat from frozen at 200°C (400°F) Mark 6 for 10-12 minutes until crisp and golden. Cut and serve as in step 7.

Peanut Chicken Skewers and Chilli Dip

Canapés with a difference, these delicate peanut-coated chicken kebabs are served with a tangy chilli and pineapple dip. The skewers freeze well, reducing last-minute preparation to the minimum, and the dip is quick to make.

Preparation time: 20 minutes, plus marinating

Cooking time: 5 minutes

Cals per skewer: 60

Makes 30

150 g (5 oz) salted peanuts	**90 ml (6 tbsp) caster sugar**
50 g (2 oz) onion	**225 g (8 oz) chicken breast fillet**
50 g (2 oz) pineapple	**1 egg white, beaten**
50 g (2 oz) cucumber	**juice of 2 limes**
1 large red chilli	**30 ml (2 tbsp) oil**
200 ml (7 fl oz) white wine vinegar	**salt and pepper**

1 Blend the peanuts in a food processor until finely chopped. Peel and finely chop the onion and pineapple. Finely chop the cucumber. Deseed and finely chop the chilli.

2 To make the chilli dip, boil the vinegar and sugar for 2 minutes and stir in the cucumber, onion, pineapple and chilli. Set aside and leave to cool.

3 Cut the chicken into 30 fine strips and toss in the beaten egg white, 30 ml (2 tbsp) lime juice, oil, salt and pepper. Set the mixture aside for 10 minutes.

4 Drain the chicken and toss in the peanuts until well coated. Thread each strip on to a wooden satay stick.

5 Grill for about 2 minutes on each side and serve hot, warm or cold with the dip.

TO FREEZE: Pack and freeze chicken only at the end of step 4.

TO USE: Thaw at cool room temperature for about 1½ hours. Make the chilli dip and complete step 5.

Spanish Meatball Tapas

These small meatballs are coated in an almond and saffron sauce – serve tapas-style with drinks.

Preparation time: 35 minutes
Cooking time: about 40 minutes
Cals per serving: 250
Makes about 30

175 g (6 oz) onion	30 ml (2 tbsp) olive oil
1 garlic clove	lemon juice, to taste
50 g (2 oz) sliced white or brown bread, crusts removed	ALMOND SAFFRON SAUCE
45 ml (3 tbsp) milk	25 g (1 oz) bread
450 g (1 lb) minced beef or lamb	2 garlic cloves
15 ml (1 tbsp) dried thyme	30 ml (2 tbsp) olive oil
30 ml (2 tbsp) chopped fresh parsley	125 g (4 oz) whole blanched almonds
5 ml (1 tsp) grated nutmeg	pinch of ground saffron
1 egg, beaten	pinch of ground cloves
salt and pepper	150 ml (¼ pint) white wine
flour for dusting	450 ml (¾ pint) chicken stock

1 Make the meatballs. Peel and finely chop the onion. Peel and crush the garlic. Soak the sliced bread in milk for 5 minutes. Squeeze out the liquid, then blend the bread with the onion, garlic, mince, thyme, parsley, nutmeg, egg and seasoning. Shape the mixture into 30 balls, then dust with flour.

2 Heat the oil in a frying pan and fry the meatballs in batches for 4-5 minutes until cooked.

3 To make the sauce, cut the bread into pieces; peel and crush the garlic. Heat the oil in the frying pan and cook the almonds and bread over a low heat until golden, stirring frequently. Stir in the garlic, saffron, cloves and wine. Season to taste. Allow to bubble for 1-2 minutes.

4 Put the almond mixture into a food processor, add half the stock and blend until almost smooth. Return to the pan with remaining stock; bring back to the boil.

5 Add the meatballs to the sauce, simmer for 25 minutes or until they are tender, stirring occasionally. Squeeze lemon juice over to taste just before serving.

TO FREEZE: Cool, pack and freeze the meatballs at the end of step 2. Cool, pack and freeze the sauce separately at the end of step 4.

TO USE: Thaw the meatballs at cool room temperature for about 4 hours. Thaw the sauce overnight at cool room temperature. Complete as in step 5.

NOTE: Make sure that you use fresh (not previously frozen) mince for this recipe.

Italian Cheese Puffs

Flavoured with Parmesan cheese and sun-dried tomatoes, these tiny puff-pastry bites can be whipped straight from the freezer into the oven for instant party food.

Preparation time: 30 minutes, plus chilling
Cooking time: 10-12 minutes
Cals per puff: 40
Makes 30

45 ml (3 tbsp) freshly grated Parmesan cheese	**flour for dusting**
30 ml (2 tbsp) sun-dried tomato paste	**225 g (8 oz) puff pastry**
5 ml (1 tsp) chopped fresh thyme	**beaten egg, to glaze**
pepper	**30 ml (2 tbsp) poppy seeds**

1 Combine the Parmesan cheese, sun-dried tomato paste, thyme and pepper in a small bowl.

2 Dust the surface with flour and roll out the pastry to a 35.5 cm (14 inch) square. Trim the edges.

3 Spread the pastry with the cheese and tomato mixture. Fold in half and gently roll out the pastry to a rectangle 18 x 35.5 cm (7 x 14 inches), about 3 mm (⅛ inch) thick, taking care not to squeeze out the filling.

4 Brush with the egg, then sprinkle generously with poppy seeds. Stamp out shapes, such as stars or hearts. Place on a baking sheet and chill for at least 1 hour.

5 Cook at 220°C (425°F) Mark 7 for 10-12 minutes or until risen and golden brown. Serve warm.

TO FREEZE: Complete to the end of step 4. Wrap and freeze.

TO USE: Cook the puffs from frozen – place on a baking sheet and cook at 200°C (400°F) Mark 6 for 10-15 minutes.

French Onion Tarts

These classic individual tarts make an elegant starter or light snack and freeze well. Serve with plum tomatoes roasted in olive oil and topped with black olives for an attractive finish.

Preparation time: 35 minutes, plus chilling
Cooking time: 1 hour 10 minutes
Cals per serving: 810
Serves 6

225 g (8 oz) plain flour	**200 g (7 oz) feta cheese**
275 g (10 oz) butter	**50 g (2 oz) Emmenthal cheese**
450 g (1 lb) large onions	**2 eggs**
salt and pepper	**TO GARNISH**
10 ml (2 tsp) chopped fresh thyme	**thyme sprigs**
150 ml (¼ pint) double cream	

1 To make the pastry, place the flour and 225 g (8 oz) butter in a food processor and process until the mixture resembles fine crumbs. Pulse the mixture, adding about 45 ml (3 tbsp) iced water, one spoonful at a time, until it forms a ball. Wrap and chill for 30 minutes.

2 Roll the pastry out on a lightly floured work surface and line six individual loose-bottomed tart tins, each with a base measurement of 8 cm (3¼ inches) and 3 cm (1¼ inches) deep. Prick the bases well and chill for 30 minutes.

3 Peel, halve and slice the onions. Melt the remaining 50 g (2 oz) butter in a large, heavy-based saucepan. Add the onions, seasoning and thyme. Cover and cook slowly over a gentle heat, stirring occasionally, for 30 minutes or until very soft and golden. Remove the lid, increase the heat and cook until all the pan juices have evaporated. Stir in the cream and leave to cool.

4 Line the pastry cases with greaseproof paper and baking beans and bake blind at 200°C (400°F) Mark 6 for 10 minutes. Remove the paper and beans and cook for a further 10 minutes or until the pastry is golden and cooked through.

5 Crumble the feta cheese, grate the Emmenthal cheese and separate the eggs. Combine the yolks and cheeses with the onion mixture and season well.

6 Whisk the egg whites until stiff, then fold into the onion mixture. Spoon the mixture into the cooked pastry cases and cook on the top shelf of the oven for 20 minutes or until the filling is risen and puffed up.

7 To serve, turn the tarts out of the tins and garnish with fresh thyme.

TO FREEZE: Cool, pack and freeze at the end of step 6.
TO USE: Reheat from frozen at 200°C (400°F) Mark 6 for 25-30 minutes, covering for the last 10 minutes.

Twice-baked Goats' Cheese Soufflés

Individual cheese soufflés, with a surprise tomato-garlic filling, are sure to impress.

Preparation time: 30 minutes, plus cooling
Cooking time: 1½ hours
Cals per serving: 425
Serves 8

2 garlic cloves	**50 g (2 oz) plain flour**
45 ml (3 tbsp) olive oil	**300 ml (½ pint) milk**
30 ml (2 tbsp) tomato purée	**4 eggs, separated**
400 g (14 oz) can chopped plum tomatoes	**225 g (8 oz) soft, creamy goats' cheese**
large sprig fresh thyme or 1.25 ml (¼ tsp) dried	**300 ml (½ pint) double cream**
salt and pepper	**TO GARNISH**
50 g (2 oz) butter, plus extra for greasing	**oakleaf lettuce or fresh herbs**

1 Peel and crush the garlic. Heat the oil in a small saucepan and add the tomato purée and garlic. Cook, stirring, for 1 minute. Add the tomatoes, thyme and seasoning. Bring to the boil, then simmer gently for 45 minutes or until the sauce is very thick. Set aside to cool.

2 Base-line and lightly butter eight 150 ml (¼ pint) ramekin dishes.

3 Melt the butter in a medium-sized saucepan and stir in the flour. Mix to a smooth paste. Blend in the milk and stir continually until the mixture boils and is smooth. Cool a little, then beat in the egg yolks and cheese. Season well. Whisk the egg whites to soft peaks and fold into the cheese mixture.

4 Fill each ramekin two-thirds full and place 10 ml (2 tsp) tomato filling in the centre of each. Cover with remaining soufflé mixture. Reserve the remaining tomato filling.

5 Place the ramekins in a roasting tin and add enough hot water to come halfway up the side of the dishes. Cook at 180°C (350°F) Mark 4 for 20 minutes or until firm to the touch. Remove from the roasting tin and cool.

6 Run a round-bladed knife around the edge of the soufflés and carefully turn out into individual ovenproof dishes.

7 Add 10 ml (2 tsp) pepper to the cream. Spoon 30-45 ml (2-3 tbsp) on top of each soufflé. Bake at 200°C (400°F) Mark 6 for 20-25 minutes or until golden. Meanwhile, reheat the remaining tomato filling. To serve, spoon a little hot tomato on top of each soufflé, garnish and serve.

TO FREEZE: Pack and freeze at the end of step 5.
TO USE: Thaw overnight in the refrigerator and complete as directed.

Gnocchi with Chilli Sauce

Potato gnocchi served with a chilli-flavoured sauce provides an interesting starter. Easy to make and freeze, the gnocchi can also be served as a light vegetarian lunch dish.

Preparation time: 1 hour
Cooking time: 40 minutes
Cals per serving: 355-235
Serves 4-6

900 g (2 lb) floury potatoes, such as King Edwards	**150 ml (¼ pint) dry white wine (optional)**
2 egg yolks	**10 ml (2 tsp) mild chilli seasoning**
90 g (3½ oz) plain white flour	**pinch of sugar**
CHILLI SAUCE	**salt and pepper**
1 onion	**TO GARNISH**
1 carrot	**freshly grated Parmesan cheese**
1 celery stick	**chopped fresh herbs**
900 g (2 lb) fresh ripe tomatoes, or two 400 g (14 oz) cans plum tomatoes with juice	

1 To make the chilli sauce, peel and chop the onion; peel and dice the carrot; trim and dice the celery. Roughly chop the tomatoes and place in a saucepan. Add all the remaining sauce ingredients to the pan, bring to the boil and simmer, half covered, for 45 minutes until very thick, stirring occasionally. Pass through a sieve or purée and sieve to remove the tomato seeds. Season with salt and pepper.

2 Peel the potatoes, then cook in salted water for 10-12 minutes until tender. Drain and leave to steam in a colander over the empty saucepan on a low heat for 1-2 minutes to dry out.

3 Press the potatoes through a sieve and cool. Add the egg yolks and flour to the potatoes and season with salt and pepper. Bring the mixture together and knead until smooth on a floured surface.

4 Roll the mixture into sausages, 2 cm (¾ inch) wide, press with a fork and cut into 2.5 cm (1 inch) lengths. Place on a floured, clean tea-towel.

5 Bring two large pans of salted water to the boil, then turn down to a simmer. Add a quarter of the gnocchi to each pan and simmer for at least 10 minutes. Lift out with a slotted spoon, draining well. Place in a warm, oiled dish, cover and keep warm while cooking the rest.

6 Reheat the sauce and serve with the gnocchi, garnished with Parmesan and herbs.

TO FREEZE: Open-freeze the uncooked gnocchi, then pack and return to the freezer. Cool the sauce and pack separately.
TO USE: Cook the gnocchi from frozen for 15 minutes. Thaw the sauce overnight at cool room temperature, then reheat to serve.

Mushroom Samosas

Deliciously spicy, these little samosas are ideal to serve at the start of an Indian-style meal.
Allow them to cool before serving, as the filling becomes very hot.

Preparation time: 40 minutes
Cooking time: 50 minutes
Cals per serving: 350
Serves 6

2.5 cm (1 inch) piece root ginger	**2.5 ml (½ tsp) ground turmeric**
125 g (4 oz) onion	**pinch of cayenne pepper**
3 garlic cloves	**salt and pepper**
30 ml (2 tbsp) natural yogurt	**125 g (4 oz) frozen petit pois**
225 g (8 oz) button mushrooms	**30 ml (2 tbsp) chopped fresh coriander**
125 g (4 oz) potato	**about 300 g (11 oz) filo pastry**
25 g (1 oz) butter	**oil for brushing**
5 ml (1 tsp) cumin seeds	

1 Peel and finely chop the ginger and onion. Peel and crush the garlic. Combine the ginger and garlic with the yogurt and set aside. Roughly chop the mushrooms; peel and finely dice the potato.

2 Heat the butter in a medium-sized saucepan. Add the onion and cook for 5-7 minutes or until soft. Add the spices and cook for 30 seconds. Add the mushrooms and cook over a high heat, stirring, for 2 minutes or until all the liquid has evaporated.

3 Add the yogurt mixture, potatoes and 150 ml (¼ pint) water. Bring to the boil. Cover and simmer, stirring occasionally, for 25-30 minutes or until the potatoes are cooked and nearly all the liquid has been absorbed. Add the peas 5 minutes before the end. Set aside to cool, then add the coriander and season with salt and pepper.

4 Cut the filo into rectangles 30.5 x 12.5 cm (12 x 5 inches). Keep covered with a damp tea-towel. Brush a rectangle lightly with oil, fold in half lengthways to form a strip 6.5 cm (2½ inches) wide and brush again with oil. Place about 10 ml (2 tsp) of the potato mixture in the bottom left-hand corner, fold the filo over to form a triangle and continue to fold until the filling is enclosed in several layers. Brush with oil. Repeat with the remaining filling and filo.

5 Cook at 200°C (400°F) Mark 6 for 10 minutes or until a deep golden brown.

TO FREEZE: Cool, pack and freeze at the end of step 5.
TO USE: Reheat from frozen at 200°C (400°F) Mark 6 for 10 minutes or until piping hot.

FISH AND SHELLFISH

Coconut Fish Curry

White fish steaks, bathed in an aromatic coconut milk sauce, is a delicious Indian-style dish. Serve with basmati rice and steamed green beans for a main course.

Preparation time: 20 minutes
Cooking time: 35 minutes
Cals per serving: 580
Serves 4

2.5 cm (1 inch) piece fresh root ginger	**2.5 ml (½ tsp) ground turmeric**
225 g (8 oz) onions	**10 ml (2 tsp) curry paste**
2 garlic cloves	**400 ml (14 fl oz) can coconut milk**
2-3 green chillies (optional)	**30 ml (2 tbsp) chopped fresh coriander**
salt and pepper	**30 ml (2 tbsp) chopped fresh mint**
700 g (1½ lb) cod or haddock steaks	**45 ml (3 tbsp) lime juice**
30 ml (2 tbsp) plain flour	**TO GARNISH**
75 ml (5 tbsp) oil	**coriander sprigs**

1 Peel and finely chop the fresh root ginger and the onions. Peel and crush the garlic. Split open the chillies, if using, removing the seeds for a milder heat. Season the fish with salt and pepper and dust lightly with the flour.

2 Heat 45 ml (3 tbsp) oil in a heavy-based casserole and fry the fish steaks in batches over a high heat for about 1-2 minutes or until well browned. Set aside.

3 Wipe out the pan and heat the remaining oil. Fry the onions with the chillies in the oil for about 10 minutes or until beginning to soften and turn golden. Add the ginger, garlic, turmeric and curry paste. Cook for a further minute.

4 Stir in the coconut milk and herbs, then simmer gently over a medium heat for 10-15 minutes or until syrupy. (The sauce can be strained at this stage to leave a smooth sauce, but this is optional.) Return the fish to heat through and cook further, if necessary.

5 Add the lime juice and serve immediately, garnished with coriander sprigs.

TO FREEZE: Complete to the end of step 4, taking care not to overcook the fish. Cool, pack and freeze.
TO USE: Thaw overnight at cool room temperature. Bring slowly to the boil, simmer for 4-5 minutes, then complete as in step 5 to serve.

Couscous Crusted Fish

The coated fish can be cooked from frozen for a very speedy supper.

Preparation time: about 1 hour, plus chilling
Cooking time: 15 minutes
Cals per serving: 435
Serves 4

2-3 large lemons	**30 ml (2 tbsp) chopped fresh flat-leaf parsley**
50 g (2 oz) couscous	**2 anchovy fillets**
4 skinless, boneless white fish steaks, about 175 g (6 oz) each	**90 ml (6 tbsp) olive oil**
salt and pepper	**15 ml (1 tbsp) capers or caper berries**
25 g (1 oz) plain flour	**450 g (1 lb) tomatoes, preferably plum**
1 egg, beaten	**TO GARNISH**
1 garlic clove	**grated lemon rind**
175 g (6 oz) pitted black olives	**sprigs of flat-leaf parsley**

1 Grate the lemon rind and squeeze the juice. There should be about 120 ml (8 tbsp) juice. Reserve 15 ml (1 tbsp) lemon juice and place the remainder in a measuring jug and add enough boiling water to make up to 175 ml (6 fl oz). Place the couscous in a bowl and pour over the warm lemon liquid. Leave for about 15 minutes until the grains have swollen and absorbed the liquid.

2 Stir in the lemon rind and season well. Spread the couscous out on a tray and place in a warm place for about 20 minutes to dry out a little.

3 Season the fish steaks. Dip each one into the flour, then the beaten egg and finally the couscous mixture. Cover lightly and chill for at least 1 hour or overnight.

4 Peel the garlic and place in a food processor with the olives, parsley, anchovy fillets, 30 ml (2 tbsp) olive oil and the reserved lemon juice. Blend for about 5 seconds; then spoon into a bowl. Add the capers and set aside.

5 Quarter the tomatoes and drizzle with 15 ml (1 tbsp) olive oil. Season well with salt and pepper.

6 Heat the remaining olive oil in a large, non-stick frying pan, and fry the fish for about 4 minutes on each side or until the crust is golden and the fish cooked. Place on a baking sheet and keep warm in a low oven.

7 Fry the tomatoes in the oil still clinging to them for 1-2 minutes. Add the olive mixture to the pan and warm through for about 1 minute. Serve with the fish steaks, garnished with grated lemon rind and parsley.

TO FREEZE: Wrap and freeze the fish at the end of step 3.
TO USE: Cook from frozen over a low heat for about 10-12 minutes on each side, and complete the recipe.

Haddock and Spinach Bake

A crunchy topping hides tender haddock, bathed in a creamy cider sauce on a bed of spinach.

Preparation time: 40 minutes
Cooking time: 25-30 minutes
Cals per serving: 817-545
Serves 4-6

350 g (12 oz) smoked haddock	**150 ml (1¼ pint) cider**
350 g (12 oz) fresh haddock	**125 g (4 oz) Gruyère cheese, grated**
300 ml (½ pint) milk	**5 ml (1 tsp) Dijon mustard**
2 bay leaves	**TOPPING**
8 peppercorns	**finely grated rind and juice of 1 lemon**
700 g (1½ lb) fresh spinach	**45 ml (3 tbsp) chopped fresh parsley**
175 g (6 oz) cherry tomatoes	**10 ml (2 tsp) sesame seeds**
75 g (3 oz) butter	**125 g (4 oz) fresh white breadcrumbs**
freshly grated nutmeg	**50 g (2 oz) toasted ground almonds**
salt and pepper	**2 egg yolks**
40 g (1½ oz) plain flour	

1 Place all the haddock skin-side up in a wide pan. Cover with the milk, add the bay leaves and peppercorns and poach gently for 10 minutes or until just opaque. Drain off and reserve the liquid. Remove the skin from the fish and break the flesh into large flakes.

2 Remove the stalks from the spinach. Wash the leaves, then place in a saucepan, cover and cook for a few minutes over a high heat until they start to wilt. Plunge into cold water to set the colour, then drain and squeeze out the moisture; roughly chop. Halve the cherry tomatoes.

3 Heat 25 g (1 oz) butter in a saucepan and add the spinach. Sauté gently for 1-2 minutes, then season with nutmeg, salt and pepper. Stir in the tomatoes. Spread in an even layer in a shallow oven dish. Arrange the cooked fish over the spinach.

4 To make the sauce, melt the remaining butter in a saucepan, add the flour and cook gently for 1-2 minutes. Whisk in the reserved cooking liquid and cider. Bring to the boil, stirring all the time, reduce the heat slightly and simmer for 10 minutes. Stir in half the cheese and the mustard. Season and pour over the fish.

5 Mix all the ingredients for the topping together with the remaining cheese. Rub in lightly until the breadcrumbs are moist. Scatter evenly over the surface.

6 Bake at 200°C (400°F) Mark 6 for 25-30 minutes until the topping is golden and crisp.

TO FREEZE: Complete to the end of step 5, cool quickly, pack and freeze.

TO USE: Thaw overnight in the refrigerator, bake as above.

Mediterranean Monkfish Stew with Lentils

A substantial fish stew which freezes well. Serve with new potatoes tossed in butter for a complete meal.

Preparation time: 35 minutes
Cooking time: 20 minutes
Cals per serving: 619
Serves 4

2 rashers streaky bacon	**150 ml (¼ pint) dry red wine**
1 small onion	**450 ml (¾ pint) fish stock**
1 carrot	**1 bay leaf**
1 celery stick	**1 small strip fresh orange rind**
2 garlic cloves	**salt and pepper**
6 sun-dried tomatoes	**700 g (1½ lb) trimmed monkfish fillets, cubed**
60 ml (4 tbsp) olive oil	**45 ml (3 tbsp) chopped fresh parsley**
350 g (12 oz) Puy lentils	

1 Dice the bacon. Peel and finely chop the onion and the carrot. Finely dice the celery. Peel and finely chop the garlic. Slice the sun-dried tomatoes.

2 Heat 30 ml (2 tbsp) olive oil in a saucepan, add the bacon and cook for 2-3 minutes until beginning to brown. Stir in the onion, carrot, celery and garlic and cook, stirring, for about 10 minutes until golden. Add the sun-dried tomatoes, lentils, wine, fish stock, bay leaf and orange rind and bring to the boil. Reduce the heat, cover tightly and simmer for 10 minutes. Season well with salt and pepper.

3 Meanwhile, heat the remaining oil in a frying pan and quickly fry the monkfish in batches, until golden on all sides, making sure the fish is not cooked through completely.

4 Stir the fish into the lentils, adding a little extra water or stock if it looks too dry, then cover and cook for 20 minutes or until the fish is tender and the lentils are very soft. Stir in the parsley and serve.

TO FREEZE: Cool the lentils completely at the end of step 2. Fry the fish as in step 3, cool completely and add to the lentils. Pack, making sure the fish is submerged in the liquid, then freeze.

TO USE: Thaw overnight in the refrigerator, then transfer to a covered saucepan, add 150 ml (¼ pint) fish stock, bring to a gentle simmer and simmer for 20 minutes until tender and heated through.

Crispy Salmon Fishcakes

These tasty little fishcakes are perfect to cook and freeze in batches. The sauce does not freeze, but can be made in less time than it takes to reheat the fishcakes!

Preparation time: 15 minutes
Cooking time: 22 minutes, plus cooling
Cals per serving: 740
Serves 6

50 g (2 oz) spring onions	2 beaten eggs
450 g (1 lb) salmon fillet	50 g (2 oz) polenta or 125 g (4 oz) breadcrumbs
150 ml (¼ pint) white wine	oil for frying
salt and pepper	HERB BUTTER SAUCE
65 g (2½ oz) butter	225 g (8 oz) unsalted butter
30 ml (2 tbsp) chopped fresh parsley	small bunch fresh chives, parsley, chervil or dill
275 g (10 oz) mashed potatoes	50 ml (2 fl oz) fish liquor (see step 3)
5-10 ml (1-2 tsp) lemon juice	30 ml (2 tbsp) lemon juice
30 ml (2 tbsp) plain flour	salt and pepper

1 Finely chop the spring onions and place in a shallow saucepan with the salmon and wine. Add enough cold water to barely cover the fish, season and bring to the boil. Take off heat, cover and leave the fish to cool completely in the liquid.

2 Drain the fish and return the liquid to the pan; set the fish aside. Add 15 g (½ oz) butter to the pan and return to the boil. Bubble furiously for about 10 minutes to reduce to a syrupy consistency.

3 Flake the salmon into a bowl, discarding skin and bones. Mix 45 ml (3 tbsp) of the reduced liquid with the parsley, mashed potatoes and lemon juice. (Freeze the remaining liquid for Herb Butter Sauce.)

4 Adjust the seasoning and shape mixture into 12 fat cakes 4 cm (1½ inches) across. Dip into the flour, egg and then polenta or breadcrumbs. Chill for 15 minutes.

5 Melt the remaining butter and brush all over the fishcakes. Cook at 240°C (475°F) Mark 9 for 20-25 minutes or until golden brown. Alternatively, shallow-fry in oil.

6 To make the sauce melt the butter and blend with all the other ingredients in a blender or food processor. Work for 1-2 minutes until creamy and smooth, then season. Serve the sauce immediately with the fishcakes.

TO FREEZE: Cool, pack and freeze at the end of step 4.
TO USE: Thaw the fish liquor. Brush the frozen fishcakes with 50 g (2 oz) melted butter as in step 5 and cook them from frozen for 25-30 minutes or until they are piping hot and golden. Cover, if necessary, towards the end of the cooking time. Complete step 6.

Salmon and Watercress Tart

For economy, smoked salmon trimmings can be used instead of smoked salmon slices.

Preparation time: 30 minutes, plus chilling
Cooking time: 1 hour
Cals per serving: 440
Serves 6

225 g (8 oz) plain flour	**225 g (8 oz) skinless salmon fillet**
1.25 ml (¼ tsp) salt	**100 ml (4 fl oz) white wine**
1.25 ml (¼ tsp) sugar	**pepper**
125 g (4 oz) unsalted butter, chilled	**125 g (4 oz) smoked salmon**
30 ml (2 tbsp) chopped fresh parsley or chives	**25 g (1 oz) watercress sprigs**
30 ml (2 tbsp) freshly grated Parmesan cheese	**150 ml (¼ pint) double cream**
3 eggs, plus 2 egg yolks	**5 ml (1 tsp) Dijon mustard**

1 Sift the flour with the salt and sugar into a food processor bowl. Add the diced butter and process for a few seconds until the mixture resembles breadcrumbs. Add the parsley or chives and grated Parmesan.

2 Add 1 beaten egg. Process in short bursts until well combined. Turn out on to a floured surface and knead gently to bring together. Wrap in cling film and chill for at least 2 hours or overnight.

3 Place the fresh salmon in a frying pan, pour the wine over and add a sprinkling of black pepper. Bring to the boil, remove from the heat, cover and leave to cool. (The fish will cook in the cooling water.) Break the cold fish into chunks, removing any bones. Roughly chop the smoked salmon and watercress.

4 Mix the watercress together with the remaining 2 eggs, 1 egg yolk, cream, mustard and pepper.

5 Roll out the pastry on a floured board and use to line a 24 cm (9½ inch) round fluted flan tin. Prick the base; chill for 20 minutes in the freezer.

6 Line the pastry case with greaseproof paper and baking beans and bake blind at 190°C (375°F) Mark 5 for 15-20 minutes. Remove the baking beans and paper and bake for a further 10 minutes or until cooked and golden.

7 Brush the warm pastry with a little of the remaining egg yolk. Place the salmon and smoked salmon on the base of the pastry case. Spoon the watercress mixture over.

8 Reduce the oven to 180°C (350°F) Mark 4. Return the tart to the oven on a baking sheet for 40 minutes or until the filling is just set. Cover with foil after 10 minutes. Leave to cool for 5 minutes before cutting.

TO FREEZE: Open-freeze at the end of step 8, then wrap and freeze again.
TO USE: Thaw for 3 hours at room temperature. Cover with foil and reheat at 190°C (375°F) Mark 5 for 10-15 minutes.

Salmon and Leek Jalousie

The top of this attractive pie is cut to resemble a Venetian blind, or jalousie in French.

Preparation time: 25 minutes
Cooking time: 35-40 minutes
Cals per serving: 820
Serves 4

350 g (12 oz) ready-made puff pastry	**50 g (2 oz) fresh breadcrumbs**
3 leeks	**50 g (2 oz) Cheddar cheese**
40 g (1½ oz) butter	**90 ml (3 fl oz) crème fraîche**
125 g (4 oz) brown cap mushrooms	**salt and pepper**
1 garlic clove	**450 g (1 lb) piece skinless salmon fillet**
15 ml (1 tbsp) chopped fresh dill	**1 egg, beaten**
5 ml (1 tsp) chopped fresh tarragon	

1 Divide the pastry into two pieces, one slightly larger than the other. Roll out the larger piece on a lightly floured surface to a rectangle, 30.5 x 20.5 cm (12 x 8 inches). Loosely fold in four, wrap in cling film and chill.

2 Roll out the smaller piece of pastry to a rectangle, measuring 25.5 x 15 cm (10 x 6 inches). Place on a dampened baking sheet and prick all over with a fork. Chill in refrigerator for 10 minutes, then bake at 230°C (450°F) Mark 8 for 10 minutes until crisp.

3 Clean and finely chop the leeks. Melt the butter in a pan, add the leeks and cook gently until soft. Roughly chop mushrooms; peel and crush the garlic.

4 Add the chopped mushrooms to the leeks with the garlic. Cook for 3 minutes, then remove from the heat and add the dill, tarragon, breadcrumbs, cheese and crème fraîche. Season with salt and pepper to taste.

5 Spread half the leek mixture on the cooked pastry, to the same dimensions as the salmon fillet. Lay the salmon on top, then spread the remaining leek mixture over the salmon.

6 Unfold the remaining pastry, lightly dust with flour and fold in half lengthways. Using a sharp knife, cut through the folded side at 5 mm (¼ inch) intervals, leaving a 5 cm (2 inch) border all the way round. Open out the rectangle.

7 Brush the edges of the cooked pastry with a little beaten egg, then lay the cut pastry rectangle on top. Press the edges together to seal, then press a fork around the edges to decorate.

8 Brush with beaten egg, and bake for 10 minutes. Lower the oven to 200°C (400°F) Mark 6 and bake for a further 15-20 minutes, until golden brown and crisp.

TO FREEZE: Pack and freeze at the end of step 7.
TO USE: Brush with beaten egg and cook from frozen at 200°C (400°F) Mark 6 for 35-40 minutes.

Fish Pie with Saffron Mash

A classic with a new twist, chunks of cod, prawns and mussels are cooked in a creamy sauce under a layer of golden coloured saffron-scented mashed potato.

Preparation time: 25 minutes
Cooking time: 30-35 minutes
Cals per serving: 845-550
Serves 4-6

½ onion	25 g (1 oz) plain flour
450 g (1 lb) cod fillet	SAFFRON MASH
450 ml (¾ pint) milk	1 kg (2¼ lb) floury potatoes
1 bay leaf	5 ml (1 tsp) saffron threads
225 g (8 oz) tomatoes	1 garlic clove
175 g (6 oz) cooked fresh prawns, peeled	75 g (3 oz) butter, melted
175 g (6 oz) cooked fresh mussels, peeled	150 ml (¼ pint) single cream
15 ml (1 tbsp) chopped fresh dill	salt and pepper
50 g (2 oz) butter	

1 To make the saffron mash, peel the potatoes and cut into chunks. Put them in a pan with enough water to cover, and add the saffron and the peeled garlic. Bring to the boil and simmer, covered, until cooked.

2 Drain the potatoes, retaining the saffron and garlic. Add the butter and mash smoothly. Add the cream and beat until light and fluffy. Season.

3 Meanwhile, peel and slice the onion. Lay the cod in an ovenproof dish, pour in the milk and add the onion and bay leaf. Cover and cook at 180°C (350°F) Mark 4 for 20 minutes until the fish is firm. Strain off the milk and reserve.

4 In the meantime, plunge the tomatoes into boiling water for 30 seconds, then refresh in cold water and peel away the skins. Cut into quarters, remove the seeds and roughly chop the flesh.

5 Flake the cod into a buttered ovenproof dish. Add the prawns, mussels and tomatoes. Scatter over the dill.

6 Melt 25 g (1 oz) butter in a pan, add the flour and cook for 30 seconds. Stir in the reserved milk, and cook, stirring, until thickened. Season with salt and pepper and pour over the fish.

7 Spoon the saffron mash on top of the fish mixture, covering it completely. Dot with the remaining butter and bake in the oven at 230°C (450°) Mark 8 for 10-15 minutes until browned on top.

TO FREEZE: Cool, pack and freeze at the end of step 7.
TO USE: Thaw at cool room temperature and reheat in the oven for 45 minutes.

Seafood Lasagne

In this rich-tasting lasagne, mixed seafood is layered with pasta, leeks and a creamy sauce.

Preparation time: 20 minutes
Cooking time: 1½ hours
Cals per serving: 720
Serves 6

450 g (1 lb) fresh haddock fillet, skinned	**90 g (3½ oz) plain flour**
300 ml (½ pint) white wine	**150 ml (¼ pint) single cream**
slices of carrot, onion and a bay leaf for flavouring	**150 ml (¼ pint) soured cream**
salt and pepper	**15 ml (1 tbsp) chopped fresh dill or 2.5 ml (½ tsp) dried**
200 g (7 oz) lasagne verde	
oil	**225 g (8 oz) fresh ready-cooked seafood cocktail or peeled, cooked prawns**
450 g (1 lb) trimmed leeks	**50 g (2 oz) Gruyère or Cheddar cheese**
1 garlic clove	**30 ml (2 tbsp) freshly grated Parmesan cheese**
150 g (5 oz) butter	**45 ml (3 tbsp) pine nuts (optional)**

1 Place the haddock fillet in a saucepan and cover with water and half the wine. Add the flavouring ingredients. Season with salt and pepper and bring to the boil. Cover and simmer for 5 minutes or until tender.

2 Flake the fish, discarding any bones. Strain the cooking juices; make up to 1 litre (1¾ pints) stock with water and reserve.

3 Cook the lasagne according to the packet instructions. Add a little oil to the water. (Even no-cook lasagne should be boiled for about 7 minutes.) Drain and run under cold water. Spread on a damp tea-towel and cover with another damp tea-towel.

4 Thickly slice the leeks. Peel and crush the garlic. Melt 50 g (2 oz) butter in a medium saucepan. Add the leeks and garlic, cover and cook for about 10 minutes. Remove using a slotted spoon.

5 Melt the remaining 75 g (3 oz) butter in the pan. Add flour and cook, stirring, for 1 minute. Off the heat, mix in the 1 litre (1¾ pints) of stock and remaining wine. Bring to the boil, stirring. Cook for 2 minutes. Off the heat, whisk in the creams and dill. Season.

6 Spoon a little of the sauce into a 3 litre (5¼ pint) shallow ovenproof dish. Top with a layer of pasta, followed by the haddock, seafood cocktail and leeks, and a little more sauce. Continue layering, finishing with the sauce. Scatter over cheeses and pine nuts if using.

7 Cook at 200°C (400°C) Mark 6 for 45-50 minutes or until piping hot and golden.

TO FREEZE: Cool, wrap and freeze at the end of step 6.
TO USE: Thaw overnight at cool room temperature. Cook as directed for 1 hour or until piping hot.

POULTRY

Fragrant Thai Curry

Chicken flavoured with exotic Thai ingredients, this dish is ideal for informal entertaining. Freezing ahead allows you more time to spend with your guests.

Preparation time: 20 minutes
Cooking time: 50 minutes
Cals per serving: 510
Serves 8

225 g (8 oz) onions	**150 ml (¼ pint) double cream**
6 garlic cloves	**60 ml (4 tbsp) mango chutney**
six 15 cm (6 inch) pieces lemon grass	**1.4 kg (3 lb) skinless chicken breast fillets**
8 kaffir lime leaves (optional)	**salt and pepper**
125 g (4 oz) creamed coconut	TO GARNISH
90 ml (6 tbsp) oil	**fresh coriander sprigs**
30 ml (2 tbsp) Thai red curry paste	**toasted cashew nuts**
150 ml (¼ pint) natural yogurt	**shredded kaffir lime leaves (optional)**

1 Peel and roughly chop the onions and garlic. Roughly chop the lemon grass and the lime leaves, if using. Dissolve the creamed coconut in 900 ml (1½ pints) boiling water.

2 Heat 45 ml (3 tbsp) oil in a large saucepan: add the onions, garlic and curry paste. Cook, stirring, for 2-3 minutes. Add the coconut milk, stirring all the time, then the lemon grass, lime leaves, yogurt, cream and chutney. Bring to the boil and simmer for 30 minutes. Blend in a food processor or blender, then sieve. Return the sauce to a clean pan.

3 Cut the chicken into fine strips. Heat the remaining oil in a large, non-stick frying pan and fry the chicken in batches for about 3-4 minutes or until cooked through. Add the chicken to the coconut sauce and bring back to the boil.

4 Adjust the seasoning and serve garnished with fresh coriander sprigs, cashew nuts and shredded kaffir lime leaves, if wished.

TO FREEZE: Cool, pack and freeze at the end of step 3.
TO USE: Thaw overnight at cool room temperature. Bring to the boil, then simmer gently for 10 minutes or until piping hot. Finish as in step 4.

Saffron Chicken with Spinach Stuffing

Freezing allows you to carry out the more time-consuming stage of stuffing and rolling the chicken ahead of time. The saffron sauce is easy to make and complements the spinach-filled chicken pieces perfectly.

Preparation time: 25 minutes

Cooking time: 1 hour

Cals per serving: 400

Serves 6

75 g (3 oz) fresh spinach or 225 g (8 oz) frozen chopped spinach, well drained	**60 ml (4 tbsp) olive oil**
25 g (1 oz) freshly grated Parmesan cheese	**125 g (4 oz) onion**
juice of 2 lemons	**1.25 ml (¼ tsp) ground saffron or 2.5 ml (½ tsp) saffron strands**
2.5 ml (½ tsp) nutmeg	**600 ml (1 pint) chicken stock**
3 garlic cloves	**150 ml (¼ pint) single cream**
salt and pepper	**TO GARNISH**
six 200 g (7 oz) skinless chicken supremes (breast with wing bone)	**roughly chopped chives**

1 Rinse, drain and dry fresh spinach. Place in a food processor with the cheese, 30 ml (2 tbsp) lemon juice, nutmeg, peeled garlic and seasoning, then blend. If using frozen spinach, simply beat together with the cheese, lemon juice, etc.

2 Using a spatula, spread the mixture over the inner side of the chicken. Roll up towards the bone. Secure with a cocktail stick.

3 Place the chicken, join side down, in a roasting tin. Squeeze over the remaining lemon juice. Add 15 ml (1 tbsp) oil. Cover with foil. Cook at 200°C (400°F) Mark 6 for about 40 minutes or until cooked.

4 Meanwhile, peel and finely chop the onion and saute in the remaining olive oil until softened. Add the saffron and cook for 1 minute. Mix in the stock. Remove from the heat.

5 When the chicken is cooked, add 75 ml (3 fl oz) of the pan juices to the saffron sauce. Bring to the boil, stir in the cream and boil for 6-7 minutes until the sauce thickens to a thin coating consistency. Season.

6 Remove the cocktail sticks and serve the chicken with the sauce spooned over. Garnish with chives.

TO FREEZE: Cover and freeze at the end of step 2.
TO USE: Thaw overnight then complete the recipe.

Parsley, Walnut and Orange Chicken

A parsley, walnut and orange stuffing is used to give roasted chicken breasts a wonderful flavour. The dish can be served either hot or cold – if serving hot, keep the chicken warm while making the dressing.

Preparation time: 15 minutes
Cooking time: 40 minutes
Cals per serving: 480
Serves 6

125 g (4 oz) onion	**1 egg, beaten**
75 g (3 oz) walnuts, shelled	**salt and pepper**
135 ml (8 tbsp) extra-virgin olive oil	**6 chicken breast fillets, with skin**
grated rind and juice of 1 large orange	**15 ml (1 tbsp) Dijon mustard**
90 ml (6 tbsp) chopped fresh parsley	**TO GARNISH**
15 ml (1 tbsp) cranberry sauce	**fresh herbs sprigs**

1 Peel and finely chop the onion; finely chop the walnuts. Heat 45 ml (3 tbsp) oil in a small saucepan and add the onion. Cover and cook for 10 minutes or until soft. Cool. In a bowl combine the walnuts, orange rind, parsley, cranberry sauce and beaten egg. Season well with salt and pepper. Stir in the cooled onion mixture. Set aside.

2 Gently ease up the chicken skin and push in the stuffing. Re-shape the chicken and place in a large roasting tin. Spread with the mustard and season. Drizzle over 30 ml (2 tbsp) oil and roast at 200°C (400°F) Mark 6 for 25-30 minutes, basting occasionally. Set aside to cool.

3 When cold, thickly slice and arrange in a serving dish. Whisk together 30 ml (2 tbsp) orange juice with the remaining olive oil and seasoning. Add the strained cooking juices and pour over the chicken. Garnish with herb sprigs and serve.

TO FREEZE: Cool, pack and freeze the chicken at the end of step 2.
TO USE: Thaw overnight at cool room temperature; to serve hot, cover and reheat in oven at 200°C (400°F) Mark 6 for 15-20 minutes.

Chicken in Cider and Honey

The part-boning of the chicken legs produces a neat shape. However, if you are short of time, you can omit the boning process, as the dish works just as well with whole chicken legs

Preparation time: 30 minutes
Cooking time: 50 minutes
Cals per serving: 300
Serves 6

6 chicken legs	**450 ml (¾ pint) medium-sweet cider**
3 Granny Smith apples	**15 ml (1 tbsp) clear honey**
juice of 1 lemon	**1 bay leaf**
225 g (8 oz) carrots	**salt and pepper**
125 g (4 oz) onion	**10 ml (2 tsp) caster sugar**
1 celery stick	**about 30 ml (2 tbsp) single cream**
65 g (2½ oz) butter	

1 If boning the chicken, with the point of a sharp knife, work the chicken flesh free from the thigh end of the legs down to the central knee joint. Sever the thigh bones at the knee joint and remove. Cut the knuckles off the drumsticks. Wrap the boned flesh down around the drumsticks and tie securely at intervals with string.

2 Peel, halve and core the apples, reserving the peel. Cut each half into three wedges. Place the apple in a bowl and toss with the lemon juice. Add enough cold water to cover and refrigerate until required. Peel and finely dice the carrots and onion; dice the celery.

3 Melt 40 g (1½ oz) butter in a shallow, flameproof casserole. Fry the chicken over a moderate heat until pale golden. Remove with a slotted spoon.

4 Stir the reserved apple peelings and vegetables into the pan. Cook, stirring, over a medium heat for 10-15 minutes until quite soft. Skim off all excess fat, then return the chicken. Add the cider, honey, bay leaf and seasoning and bring to the boil. Cover and cook at 200°C

(400°F) Mark 6 for about 30 minutes until the vegetables are very tender and the chicken is cooked.

5 Meanwhile, melt 25 g (1 oz) butter in a sauté pan and fry the drained apple with the sugar until golden.

6 Remove the chicken, remove the string and keep warm. Remove the bay leaf, then purée the contents of the casserole. Sieve into the rinsed casserole and boil for a few minutes to reduce slightly, if necessary. Take off heat.

7 Stir in the cream, adjust the seasoning and warm slightly; do not boil. Pour over the chicken. Serve with the apple.

TO FREEZE: Cool, pack and freeze together at the end of step 6. Do not cook and freeze the apple wedges.
TO USE: Thaw overnight at cool room temperature. Bring the chicken and sauce to the boil. Simmer gently for 10-15 minutes or until hot all the way through. Complete.

Provençal Chicken Bake

Chunks of chicken and pasta shapes are baked in a mouthwatering combination of tomato and pesto flavoured sauces to create a marvellous all-in-one dish.

Preparation time: 30 minutes
Cooking time: 1¾ hours
Cals per serving: 515

Serves 8

225 g (8 oz) dried pasta shells, such as orecchiette	**15 ml (1 tbsp) caster sugar**
salt and pepper	**700 g (1½ lb) skinless chicken breast fillets or boned chicken thighs**
225 g (8 oz) onions	**25 g (1 oz) butter**
2 garlic cloves	**25 g (1 oz) plain flour**
45 ml (3 tbsp) olive oil	**450 ml (¾ pint) milk**
15 ml (1 tbsp) dried thyme	**200 g (7 oz) full-fat soft cheese**
150 ml (¼ pint) dry white vermouth or white wine	**50 g (2 oz) pitted black olives**
two 400 g (14 oz) cans chopped tomatoes	**75 ml (5 tbsp) pesto sauce**
550 g (1¼ lb) tomato passata	

1 Cook the pasta in boiling, salted water until just tender. Drain, run under cold water and set aside.

2 Peel and roughly chop the onions; peel and crush the garlic. Heat 15 ml (1 tbsp) olive oil in a large saucepan, add the onions, garlic and thyme, then cook for 1-2 minutes. Pour in the dry vermouth and bubble for 2-3 minutes. Add the tomatoes, passata, seasoning and sugar. Bring to the boil and simmer for 15-20 minutes or until reduced by one-third.

3 Cut the chicken into chunks. Place in a roasting tin. Drizzle over the remaining olive oil and season. Cover with foil and cook at 200°C (400°F) Mark 6 for 10-15 minutes or until just cooked. (Take care not to overcook the chicken as it may become stringy when it is cooked again in step 6.)

4 Melt the butter in a saucepan and stir in the flour. Cook, stirring, for 1 minute then gradually add the milk and whisk until smooth. Bring to the boil, then simmer for a further 10-15 minutes, stirring occasionally. Remove from heat and whisk in the full-fat cheese; season.

5 Mix together the chicken, pasta, olives and tomato sauce and spoon into a 3.4 litre (6 pint) dish with a depth of about 4 cm (1½ inches). Lightly stir the pesto into the white sauce, to create a marbled effect. Spoon the white sauce over the chicken mixture.

6 Cook at 200°C (400°F) Mark 6 for 30-35 minutes or until golden and hot through.

TO FREEZE: Cool, wrap and freeze at the end of step 5.
TO USE: Thaw overnight at cool room temperature. Cook as in step 6 for about 45-50 minutes.

Chicken with Grapes and Madeira

This dish is delicious accompanied by potatoes and parsnips roasted in the oven until crispy, then lightly mashed together.

Preparation time: 15 minutes
Cooking time: 2 hours
Cals per serving: 440
Serves 6

6 chicken quarters (breast and wing)	**600 ml (1 pint) chicken stock**
2 shallots	**125 g (4 oz) toasted walnut halves**
15 ml (1 tbsp) oil	**salt and pepper**
50 g (2 oz) butter	**350 g (12 oz) seedless white grapes**
grated rind and juice of 2 oranges	**45 ml (3 tbsp) cornflour**
150 ml (¼ pint) dry white wine	**45 ml (3 tbsp) chopped fresh parsley**
50 ml (2 fl oz) Madeira	

1 Using sharp scissors, halve the chicken pieces. Peel and finely chop the shallots. Heat the oil and butter in a 5.1 litre (9 pint) flameproof casserole. Brown the chicken in batches, removing each batch with a slotted spoon. Drain on kitchen paper

2 Lower the heat and add the shallots. Sauté, stirring, until soft. Add the orange rind and about 150 ml (¼ pint) orange juice, the wine, Madeira, stock, walnuts and salt and pepper.

3 Return the chicken to the casserole, bring to the boil, cover and cook at 170°C (325°F) Mark 3 for 1 hour. Stir in the grapes, cover and cook for a further 30 minutes or until the chicken is tender. Remove the chicken from the casserole, trim and keep warm.

4 Blend the cornflour to a smooth paste with a little water. Add to the casserole and bring to the boil, stirring, until the juices are lightly thickened. Return the chicken to the casserole and stir in the parsley; adjust the seasoning and serve.

TO FREEZE: Cook for 1 hour only at step 3, without adding the grapes. Cool, pack and freeze.

TO USE: Thaw overnight at cool room temperature. Add the grapes and bring to the boil. Reheat at 170°C (325°F) Mark 3 for 30-40 minutes or until hot through. Finish as in step 4.

Chicken and Pepper Casserole

A very versatile dish, this chicken casserole also includes salami sausage to give extra bite.
A perfect main course for both family and friends.

Preparation time: 20 minutes
Cooking time: about 1 hour
Cals per serving: 670
Serves 4

8 small chicken joints, or 1 chicken, 1.6 kg (3½ lb), jointed	**two 400 g (14 oz) cans plum tomatoes**
salt and pepper	**150 ml (¼ pint) dry white wine**
1 onion	**30 ml (2 tbsp) chopped parsley**
4 large or 8 small shallots	**2 fresh rosemary sprigs**
2 garlic cloves	**1 strip of orange peel**
225 g (8 oz) salami sausage	**2 red peppers, or 1 red and 1 yellow pepper**
45 ml (3 tbsp) olive oil	**TO GARNISH**
	sprigs of rosemary

1 Season the chicken joints with salt and pepper. Peel and chop the onion. Peel the shallots. Peel and slice the garlic. Slice the salami sausage.

2 Heat the oil in a large, heavy-based sauté pan (which has a lid). Add the chicken pieces and brown on all sides over a fairly high heat. Transfer to a plate, cover and set aside.

3 Add the onion and whole shallots to the sauté pan and cook over a medium heat, stirring frequently, for about 10 minutes until the onion is soft and golden and the shallots are lightly browned. Stir in the garlic and salami sausage and continue cooking for 3-4 minutes until the juices begin to run from the salami sausage.

4 Meanwhile, drain the tomatoes, reserving the juice, and roughly chop. Add the wine and herbs to the pan, together with the orange peel and tomatoes with their juice. Return the chicken to the pan. Bring to the boil, lower the heat, cover and simmer for 40-45 minutes until the chicken is tender.

5 Meanwhile, halve and deseed the peppers, then grill skin-side up for about 10 minutes until the skins are blistered and blackened all over. Place the peppers in a bowl, cover and cool slightly, then peel away the skins. Cut the flesh into thin strips. Add to the chicken in the pan 5 minutes before the end of the cooking time.

6 Lift out the chicken pieces using a slotted spoon, and set aside. Increase the heat and boil steadily for a few minutes to reduce and thicken the sauce, then return the chicken to the pan. Season, garnish and serve.

TO FREEZE: Cool, pack and freeze at the end of step 5.
TO USE: Thaw overnight at cool room temperature. Complete step 6, simmering the chicken in the reduced sauce for 10-12 minutes until piping hot.

Easy Chicken Pie

For a faster topping that needs no rolling out, try this idea of grating chilled shortcrust pastry over the filling. The trick is to use ready-made pastry – the homemade version is too soft to grate.

Preparation time: 20 minutes, plus chilling
Cooking time: 45 minutes
Cals per serving: 800
Serves 4

450 g (1 lb) trimmed leeks	**150 ml (¼ pint) single cream**
350 g (12 oz) cooked chicken	**150 ml (¼ pint) white wine**
175 g (6 oz) piece lightly smoked, cooked ham	**5 ml (1 tsp) English mustard**
1 bunch watercress	**grated rind and juice of 1 lemon**
75 g (3 oz) butter	**salt and pepper**
50 g (2 oz) plain white flour	**225 g (8 oz) ready-made shortcrust pastry, well chilled**
300 ml (½ pint) chicken stock	**50 g (2 oz) Gruyère cheese**

1 Clean and thickly slice the leeks. Cut the chicken and ham into even-sized pieces. Chop the watercress.

2 Melt the butter in a pan and sauté the leeks for 5 minutes until they start to colour. Off the heat, stir in the flour. Add the stock, cream and wine, stirring continuously. Bring to the boil, then simmer gently for 3-4 minutes. Add the mustard, lemon rind and 15 ml (1 tbsp) lemon juice, the watercress, chicken, ham and salt and pepper to taste. Spoon into a 1.7 litre (3 pint) ovenproof dish.

3 Coarsely grate the chilled pastry and Gruyère cheese. Using two forks, toss lightly with pepper. Sprinkle over the chicken mixture.

4 Bake at 200°C (400°F) Mark 6 for about 35 minutes or until golden brown and piping hot.

TO FREEZE: Cool, overwrap and freeze at the end of step 3. **TO USE:** Thaw overnight at cool room temperature. Cook as in step 4, until piping hot.

Brandied Duck Terrine with Apple

Don't be put off by the length of the recipe, it's easy to prepare and freezes well.
Ideal fare for a buffet party.

Preparation time: 1½ hours, plus marinating
Cooking time: 2¼ hours
Cals per serving: 150
Serves 12

50 g (2 oz) pitted prunes	350 g (12 oz) eating apples
50 g (2 oz) dried apricots	50 g (2 oz) butter
90 ml (6 tbsp) brandy	225 g (8 oz) minced pork
350 g (12 oz) turkey breast fillet	30 ml (2 tbsp) chopped fresh thyme
800 g (1¾ lb) duck breast fillets	1 egg
a few thyme sprigs	50 g (2 oz) shelled pistachio nuts
225 g (8 oz) shallots or onions	salt and pepper

1 Roughly chop the prunes and apricots. Place in a bowl with 60 ml (4 tbsp) brandy, cover and leave overnight. Cut the turkey into 2.5 cm (1 inch) cubes. Skin the duck breasts; there should be 500 g (1 lb 2 oz) meat. Place both in a roasting tin with the thyme and remaining brandy. Cover and marinate in the refrigerator overnight.

2 Peel and roughly chop the shallots. Peel, core and chop the apples. Melt the butter in a saucepan, add the shallots and cook for 10 minutes or until soft. Stir in the apple. Cover and cook for 5-10 minutes or until soft. Set aside to cool.

3 Remove the turkey from the marinade and place in a food processor with the pork and the apple mixture. Process to a rough purée, then combine with the thyme, beaten egg, marinated fruits and nuts. Season well.

4 Remove the duck from the marinade and place between sheets of greaseproof paper. Flatten gently with a rolling pin until 1 cm (½ inch) thick.

5 Base-line a 1.1 litre (2 pint) terrine or loaf tin with greaseproof paper or foil. Place a duck breast in the base of the terrine, to cover it evenly with no gaps. Spread over half of the stuffing; repeat the process, finishing with a layer of duck.

6 Cover with foil and place in a roasting tin. Add enough hot water to come three-quarters of the way up the sides of the terrine. Cook at 180°C (350°F) Mark 4 for 2-2¼ hours or until the juices run clear when tested with a skewer. Transfer to a wire rack, cover with a weighted board. When cool, chill overnight.

7 Run a knife around the terrine; turn on to a board. Remove the greaseproof paper and carve into thin slices.

TO FREEZE: Cover and freeze at the end of step 6.
TO USE: Thaw at cool room temperature overnight. Serve as in step 7.

Duck with Caramelised Lemon Sauce

Rubbing the duck breast with a little salt draws the fat out and makes the skin attractively crisp. The sauce freezes well and the duck is simplicity itself to cook.

Preparation time: 25 minutes
Cooking time: about 1 hour 10 minutes
Cals per serving: 487
Serves 8

5 cm (2 inch) piece fresh root ginger	**150 ml (¼ pint) whipping cream**
eight 15 cm (6 inch) pieces lemon grass	**salt and pepper**
60 ml (4 tbsp) golden syrup	**30 ml (2 tbsp) chopped fresh coriander**
120 ml (8 tbsp) white wine vinegar	**8 duck breast fillets, about 175 g (6 oz) each**
120 ml (8 tbsp) light soy sauce	**TO GARNISH**
900 ml (1½ pints) chicken stock	**coriander sprigs**
60 ml (4 tbsp) brandy	

1 Peel the ginger. Roughly chop the peelings and the lemon grass for the sauce. Cut the remaining ginger flesh into very fine strips. Cook the ginger strips in boiling water for 1 minute. Drain and refresh in cold water.

2 To make the sauce, boil the syrup in a small, heavy-based pan for about 2-3 minutes until a dark caramel colour. Add the wine vinegar and bubble until reduced by half. Add the ginger peelings, lemon grass, soy sauce, stock, brandy and cream. Bring to the boil, then simmer, uncovered, for 40 minutes and strain. Stir in the ginger strips, season with salt and pepper and set aside.

3 Prick the skin of the duck breasts with a fork, then rub with salt and pepper. Brown the duck breasts, skin side down only, in a non-stick frying pan. Transfer to a roasting tin and cook at 200°C (400°F) Mark 6 for 10 minutes for medium rare or 20 minutes for well done.

4 Remove the duck breasts from the oven. Skim the duck juices of any fat and add to the reheated sauce with the chopped fresh coriander. Serve the duck with the sauce and garnish with coriander sprigs.

TO FREEZE: Prepare and cook the lemon sauce to the end of step 2. Cool, cover and freeze.
TO USE: Thaw the sauce overnight in the refrigerator. Stir over a gentle heat until bubbling. Complete steps 3 and 4.

Christmas Pheasant

Cranberries, chestnuts and Madeira give this dish a festive air. For easy preparation, use vacuum-packed cooked chestnuts. If using fresh chestnuts, buy 450 g (1 lb) to allow for wastage.

Preparation time: 30 minutes
Cooking time: 2¼ hours
Cals per serving: 490
Serves 6

225 g (8 oz) shallots or small onions	**sprig of fresh thyme or pinch of dried**
225 g (8 oz) streaky bacon	**2 bay leaves**
2 garlic cloves	**6 juniper berries**
brace of oven-ready pheasants	**pared rind and juice of 1 orange**
salt and pepper	**90 ml (6 tbsp) redcurrant jelly**
30 ml (2 tbsp) oil	**225 g (8 oz) fresh cranberries**
50 g (2 oz) butter	**225 g (8 oz) cooked chestnuts**
300 ml (½ pint) Madeira	**TO GARNISH**
600 ml (1 pint) beef stock	**fresh thyme**

1 Peel the shallots and chop the bacon. Peel and crush the garlic. Joint both pheasants into four, discarding backbone and knuckles. Season with salt and pepper.

2 Heat the oil and butter in a large, flameproof casserole and brown the shallots and bacon. Remove with a slotted spoon and set aside. Add the pheasant, half at a time, and fry for 5-6 minutes or until golden. Remove the pheasant from the casserole.

3 Stir in the crushed garlic, half the Madeira, the stock, thyme, bay leaves, juniper berries and pared orange rind. Bring to the boil, add the pheasant. Cover and cook at 170°C (325°F) Mark 3 for 1 hour.

4 Add the shallots, bacon and redcurrant jelly. Re-cover and return to the oven for 45 minutes or until the pheasant is quite tender.

5 Meanwhile, marinate the cranberries and chestnuts in the remaining Madeira and the orange juice for 30 minutes.

6 Remove the pheasant, vegetables and bacon from the liquid, cover and keep warm. Bubble the sauce for about 5 minutes to reduce to a syrupy consistency. Add the cranberry and chestnut mixture and simmer for a further 5 minutes. Adjust the seasoning and spoon this sauce over the pheasant. Serve garnished with fresh thyme.

TO FREEZE: Cool, pack and freeze at the end of step 4.
TO USE: Thaw overnight at cool room temperature. Bring to the boil, cover and cook at 180°C (350°F) Mark 4 for about 40 minutes. Complete as above.

MEAT

Beef Gulasch

In this easy-to-make dish the beef is cooked in a paprika-flavoured tomato sauce until meltingly tender, then topped with soured cream to serve. Delicious with pasta noodles.

Preparation time: 30 minutes
Cooking time: 2½ hours
Cals per serving: 525
Serves 6

700 g (1½ lb) onions	**60 ml (4 tbsp) paprika**
2 garlic cloves	**30 ml (2 tbsp) each chopped fresh thyme, parsley and rosemary, or 10 ml (2 tsp) mixed dried herbs**
225 g (8 oz) pancetta, or thick-cut, rindless streaky bacon	**400 g (14 oz) can plum tomatoes**
900 g (2 lb) stewing steak	**150 ml (¼ pint) soured cream**
salt and pepper	**TO GARNISH**
30 ml (2 tbsp) plain flour	**chopped fresh parsley**
45 ml (3 tbsp) oil	

1 Peel and roughly chop the onions. Peel and crush the garlic. Chop the pancetta into cubes. Cut the stewing steak into chunks. Season the flour with salt and pepper and toss in the meat.

2 Heat 15 ml (1 tbsp) oil in a deep, flameproof casserole and fry the onions until starting to soften and turn golden. Remove with a slotted spoon. Fry the pancetta over a high heat until crispy and remove. Heat the remaining oil with the pancetta fat and fry the steak in small batches until browned.

3 Return the onions and the pancetta to the casserole, with all the steak. Stir in crushed garlic and paprika. Cook, stirring, for 1 minute.

4 Add the herbs, tomatoes and 300 ml (½ pint) water. Bring to the boil and cook, covered, at 170°C (325°F) Mark 3 for 1½-2 hours or until tender. Check after 1 hour, adding a little water if the gulasch looks dry.

5 Adjust the seasoning, then stir in the cream. Garnish with parsley and serve.

TO FREEZE: Cool, pack and freeze at the end of step 4.
TO USE: Thaw overnight at cool room temperature. Add 150 ml (¼ pint) water. Bring to the boil in a flameproof casserole, then reheat in the oven at 150°C (300°F) Mark 2 for about 30 minutes. Complete as in step 5.

Beef in Coconut Milk

Beef seeped in coconut milk flavoured with a chilli and ginger paste is sure to be popular with anyone who enjoys spicy meals. Serve with Thai fragrant rice to mop up the juices.

Preparation time: 15 minutes
Cooking time: 1½-1¾ hours
Cals per serving: 460
Serves 6

2 large red chillies	**5 ml (1 tsp) ground cloves**
1 small red pepper	**1.6 litres (2¾ pints) coconut milk**
2.5 cm (1 inch) piece fresh root ginger	**3 bay leaves**
225 g (8 oz) shallots or onions	**900 g (2 lb) cubed stewing beef**
8 garlic cloves	**salt and pepper**
two 15 cm (6 inch) pieces lemon grass	TO GARNISH
8 kaffir lime leaves or the grated rind of 1 lime	**shredded kaffir lime leaves**
5 ml (1 tsp) ground cinnamon	**toasted coconut flakes**

1 Deseed and finely chop the chillies and red pepper. Peel the ginger, shallots and garlic and roughly chop with the lemon grass and lime leaves. Blend in a processor with the cinnamon, cloves and 150 ml (¼ pint) water until smooth.

2 Place this paste in a large non-stick saucepan with coconut milk, bay leaves and beef. Season well with salt, then bring to the boil, stirring. Simmer, uncovered, stirring occasionally, for 1½-1¾ hours until the meat is tender and the milk absorbed to make a thick coating.

3 Garnish with the lime leaves and toasted coconut flakes and serve.

TO FREEZE: Cool, pack and freeze at the end of step 2.
TO USE: Thaw overnight at cool room temperature. Add 150 ml (¼ pint) beef stock. Bring to the boil, cover and reheat at 200°C (400°F) Mark 6 for about 20-30 minutes or until piping hot.

Rich Beef Daube

This dish involves a lot of ingredients but the preparation is quick. Remember, button onions are much easier to peel if soaked in boiling water for a minute or two.

Preparation time: 35 minutes, plus soaking

Cooking time: 2½ hours

Cals per serving: 540

Serves 6

---

20 g (¾ oz) dried wild mushrooms, such as porcini or ceps

2.5 cm (1 inch) piece fresh root ginger

2 large garlic cloves

125 g (4 oz) sun-dried tomatoes

225 g (8 oz) button onions

900 g (2 lb) stewing steak

salt and pepper

1-2 large oranges

90 ml (6 tbsp) oil

45 ml (3 tbsp) plain flour

10 ml (2 tsp) dried mixed herbs

300 ml (½ pint) each red wine and beef stock

10 ml (2 tsp) caster sugar

225 g (8 oz) brown-cap mushrooms

125 g (4 oz) pitted black olives

---

1 Rinse the wild mushrooms, then soak in 150 ml (¼ pint) water for 1 hour. Peel and chop the ginger; peel and crush the garlic; chop sun-dried tomatoes. Peel the onions, leaving the root end intact, but trim to neaten. Cut the stewing steak into 2.5 cm (1 inch) cubes. Season with salt and pepper.

2 Pare the rind of 1 orange, then squeeze 100 ml (4fl oz) juice from both the oranges.

3 Heat 45 ml (3 tbsp) oil in a large flameproof casserole and brown the meat in batches over a fairly brisk heat. Remove from casserole with a slotted spoon.

4 Add 15 ml (1 tbsp) oil to the pan and fry the onions for about 7-10 minutes until golden. Return all the meat to the casserole and stir in the flour, crushed garlic, ginger, sun-dried tomatoes and herbs. Cook, stirring, for 1 minute.

5 Add the wild mushrooms with the soaking liquid, the wine, stock, pared orange rind, the orange juice and the sugar. Bring to the boil, then cover and cook at 170°C (325°F) Mark 3 for about 2 hours or until very tender.

6 Heat the remaining oil in a frying pan, cook the brown-cap mushrooms briskly over a high heat, then add them to the casserole. Remove the orange rind and add the olives. Return the casserole to the oven for another 15-20 minutes. Adjust the seasoning and serve.

TO FREEZE: Cool, pack and freeze at the end of step 5.
TO USE: Thaw overnight in the refrigerator. Stir over a gentle heat until just boiling. Add a drop of water if the sauce is too concentrated. Then add the mushrooms and olives and simmer gently for a further 5 minutes. Season and serve.

Steak and Kidney Pudding

Freezing the filling ahead of time makes this traditional savoury pudding easier to prepare.

Preparation time: 20 minutes, plus cooling

Cooking time: 3½-4 hours

Cals per serving: 610

Serves 6

700 g (1½ lb) stewing steak	**60 ml (4 tbsp) chopped fresh parsley**
225 g (8 oz) ox kidney	**275 g (10 oz) white self-raising flour**
225 g (8 oz) onion	**150 g (5 oz) shredded suet**
about 45 ml (3 tbsp) oil	**grated rind of 1 lemon**
45 ml (3 tbsp) plain white flour	**butter for greasing**
600 ml (1 pint) beef stock	**TO GARNISH**
15 ml (1 tbsp) wholegrain mustard	**flat-leaf parsley**
salt and pepper	

1 Cut the stewing steak and ox kidney into large, bite-sized pieces. Peel and chop the onion.

2 Heat 45 ml (3 tbsp) oil in a flameproof casserole and brown the steak and kidney in batches, adding more oil if necessary. Remove and drain on kitchen paper.

3 Add the onion to the casserole and lightly brown. Off the heat, stir in the plain flour, stock, mustard and salt and pepper. Bring to the boil, then return the steak and kidney to the casserole.

4 Cover the casserole and cook at 170°C (325°F) Mark 3 for 2 hours or until the meat is tender. Adjust the seasoning, stir in the parsley and cool.

5 Mix together the self-raising flour, suet, lemon rind and seasoning. Bind to a soft dough with about 175-200 ml (6-7 fl oz) water. Knead lightly until just smooth.

6 Roll out the dough to a 33 cm (13 inch) round. Cut out one quarter and reserve. Line a 1.7 litre (3 pint) greased pudding basin with the large piece of dough, damping and overlapping the join to seal.

7 Spoon in the meat and juices. Roll out the reserved dough and use to top the pudding, damping the pastry edges to seal. Trim to neaten.

8 Cover the basin with greased and pleated greaseproof paper and foil; tie securely with string.

9 Place in a pan, standing the basin on a heatproof saucer. Pour boiling water around the basin to come halfway up the sides. Cover tightly. Boil for 1½-2 hours, topping up as necessary. Garnish with parsley.

TO FREEZE: Pack and freeze at the end of step 4.

TO USE: Thaw overnight at cool room temperature and complete as above from step 5.

Beef with Vegetable Topping

A mixture of root vegetables combined with Cheddar cheese and mayonnaise makes a wonderful topping for minced beef.

Preparation time: 10 minutes
Cooking time: 1 hour
Cals per serving: 570
Serves 6

1 large onion	**600 ml (1 pint) beef stock**
1 large carrot	**salt and pepper**
30 ml (2 tbsp) oil	**30 ml (2 tbsp) chopped fresh parsley**
900 g (2 lb) minced beef	**TOPPING**
30 ml (2 tbsp) plain flour	**1.1 kg (2½ lb) mixed root vegetables, such as parsnips, turnips, potatoes**
2.5 ml (½ tsp) ground cinnamon	**45-60 ml (3-4 tbsp) mayonnaise**
30 ml (2 tbsp) tomato purée	**75 g (3 oz) mature Cheddar cheese, grated**
5 ml (1 tsp) dried thyme	**melted butter for brushing**

1 Peel and chop the onion and carrot. Heat half the oil in a large flameproof casserole and fry the mince over a high heat, stirring occasionally, until the meat is a caramel brown colour. Lift out and set aside.

2 Heat the remaining oil and fry the carrot and onion over a high heat for 5 minutes or until starting to soften.

3 Return the mince to the casserole. Add the flour, cinnamon and tomato purée and cook for 1 minute. Stir in the thyme, stock and salt and pepper. Bring to the boil. Put in the oven at 180°C (350°F) Mark 4 for 40 minutes. Skim off the fat, add the parsley and adjust seasoning.

4 For the topping, peel the root vegetables and cut into chunks. Cover with cold, salted water and bring to the boil. Simmer for 20 minutes or until very soft. Drain

and dry well (see note). Mash the vegetables, leaving some chunks for texture. Stir in the mayonnaise and cheese. Season with salt and pepper.

5 Spoon the mince into a deep 23 cm (9 inch) square ovenproof baking dish, pile the mash on top and brush with melted butter.

6 Place the dish on a baking tray. Cook at 200°C (400°F) Mark 6 for 20-25 minutes or until golden.

TO FREEZE: Cool, wrap and freeze at the end of step 5.
TO USE: Thaw overnight at cool room temperature. Complete as in step 6, allowing 30-35 minutes cooking.

NOTE: For a crisp topping, put the drained vegetables back in the pan over a low heat. Crush and stir in the pan to drive off the steam before adding the mayonnaise.

Chilli with Potato Wedges

A warming family supper dish, perfect for chilly Autumn evenings. Potato wedges and lots of soured cream and cheese are the ideal accompaniments.

Preparation time: 20 minutes
Cooking time: 1½ hours
Cals per serving: 700
Serves 6

225 g (8 oz) onions	**10 ml (2 tsp) dark soft brown sugar**
3 celery sticks	**30 ml (2 tbsp) Worcestershire sauce**
2 red chillies	**15 ml (1 tbsp) dried oregano**
400 g (14 oz) can red kidney beans	**300 ml (½ pint) beef stock**
75 ml (5 tbsp) olive oil	**two 400 g (14 oz) cans chopped tomatoes**
900 g (2 lb) minced beef	**1.1 kg (2½ lb) potatoes**
5-10 ml (1-2 tsp) hot chilli powder, to taste	**TO SERVE**
5 ml (1 tsp) ground cumin	**soured cream**
15 ml (1 tbsp) tomato purée	**grated Cheddar cheese**

1 Peel and finely chop the onion; finely chop the celery sticks. Deseed and finely chop the chillies. Drain and rinse the red kidney beans.

2 Heat 30 ml (2 tbsp) olive oil in a large casserole, then add the onion, celery and chillies. Fry over a medium heat for about 10 minutes or until the onion is beginning to soften.

3 Increase the heat, add the mince and fry for a further 10-15 minutes or until the meat is beginning to turn golden brown. Stir in the hot chilli powder, ground cumin and tomato purée. Fry for a further minute.

4 Add the soft brown sugar, Worcestershire sauce, oregano, beef stock, chopped tomatoes and the drained kidney beans. Bring to the boil. Cover the casserole tightly and place the chilli on the lower shelf of the oven at 190°C (375°F) Mark 5 for 20 minutes.

5 Cut the scrubbed potatoes into wedges and toss in the remaining olive oil. Place in a roasting tin and season with plenty of salt and pepper.

6 Place the potato wedges on the top shelf and cook for 35 minutes or until the meat is tender and the potatoes are golden. Skim off the fat from the chilli.

7 Serve the chilli in bowls topped with soured cream and grated cheese. Accompany with the potatoes.

TO FREEZE: Prepare to the end of step 6. Cool, pack and freeze the chilli and cooked potato wedges separately

TO USE: Thaw overnight at cool room temperature. Reheat the chilli on the hob, bring to the boil and simmer for 10 minutes. Place the potato wedges on a baking sheet and reheat at 230°C (450°F) Mark 8 for 10-12 minutes. Serve as directed.

Lamb Tagine with Dates

Lamb is cooked with pungent spices and sweet fruit to make a delicious party dish that is bursting with Middle Eastern flavours. Couscous is the ideal accompaniment.

Preparation time: 30 minutes, plus chilling

Cooking time: 1½ hours

Cals per serving: 585

Serves 10

1.4 kg (3 lb) boneless lamb, leg or shoulder	**30 ml (2 tbsp) chopped fresh parsley**
10 ml (2 tsp) each ground ginger and coriander	**450 ml (¾ pint) chicken stock**
2.5 ml (½ tsp) saffron strands	**150 ml (¼ pint) sherry**
75 ml (5 tbsp) olive oil	**1 cinnamon stick**
salt and pepper	**1 bay leaf**
275 g (10 oz) pearl onions or shallots	**75 g (3 oz) stoned dates**
1 garlic clove	**15 ml (1 tbsp) honey**
15 ml (1 tbsp) plain flour	**TO GARNISH**
15 ml (1 tbsp) tomato purée	**coriander sprigs**
30 ml (2 tbsp) chopped fresh coriander	

1 Cut the lamb into large cubes, place in a bowl with the ginger, ground coriander, saffron strands, and 15 ml (1 tbsp) oil. Season with salt and pepper, cover and chill overnight.

2 Put the onions in boiling water for 2 minutes, drain, rinse under cold water and peel. Peel and crush the garlic. Heat 15 ml (1 tbsp) oil in a heavy-based casserole and brown the lamb in batches, using more oil when necessary. Add the garlic and stir over heat for 1 minute.

3 Return the lamb to the casserole with the onions, flour, tomato purée, fresh coriander, parsley, chicken stock, sherry, cinnamon stick and bay leaf. Season. Bring to the boil, cover and cook in the oven at 190°C (375°F) Mark 5 for 1¼ hours, stirring occasionally.

4 Discard the cinnamon stick and bay leaf. Add the dates and honey, return to the oven for 15-20 minutes. Garnish with coriander and serve.

TO FREEZE: Cool, pack and freeze at the end of step 4.
TO USE: Thaw overnight at cool room temperature. Add 150 ml (¼ pint) stock and bring to the boil. Reheat gently at 180°C (350°F) Mark 4 for 30 minutes.

Italian Lamb

Look out for bags of dried porcini pieces in supermarkets. They're chopped dried mushrooms which are ideal for adding a rich depth of flavour to stews or casseroles.

Preparation time: 35 minutes
Cooking time: 3¾ hours
Cals per serving: 660
Serves 6

2 half leg knuckles of lamb	**600 ml (1 pint) red wine**
30 ml (2 tbsp) olive oil	**400 g (14 oz) tomato passata**
275 g (10 oz) onions	**600 ml (1 pint) vegetable stock**
175 g (6 oz) each carrots and celery	**125 g (4 oz) dried pasta shapes**
9 pieces sun-dried tomato	**15 g (½ oz) freshly grated Parmesan cheese**
150 g (5 oz) Italian-style spicy or salami sausage	**TO GARNISH**
75 g (3 oz) butter	**flat-leaf parsley**
30 ml (2 tbsp) dried porcini pieces or 125 g (4 oz) finely chopped brown-cap mushrooms	

1 Place the lamb in a large roasting tin and drizzle over 15 ml (1 tbsp) oil. Roast at 240°C (475°F) Mark 9 for 35 minutes.

2 Meanwhile, peel and finely chop the onions and carrots. Finely chop the celery and sun-dried tomatoes. Thickly slice the sausage. Melt the butter with the remaining oil in a large flameproof casserole. Stir in the vegetables and cook, stirring, for 10-15 minutes or until golden and soft. Stir in the porcini pieces or finely chopped brown-cap mushrooms and cook for a further 2-3 minutes.

3 Add the sun-dried tomatoes and sausage to the pan with the wine, passata and stock. Bring to the boil and simmer for 10 minutes.

4 Lift the lamb from the roasting tin and add to the tomato sauce; cover with a tight-fitting lid. Reduce the oven temperature to 170°C (325°F) Mark 3 and cook for a further 3 hours or until lamb is falling off the bone.

5 Lift the lamb from the casserole on to a deep, heatproof platter. Cover loosely with foil and keep warm in a low oven.

6 Place the casserole on the hob, stir in the pasta and return to the boil. Simmer for 10 minutes or until the pasta is tender. Stir in the Parmesan just before serving.

7 Serve the lamb carved into large pieces with the pasta sauce. Garnish with parsley.

TO FREEZE: Cool, pack and freeze at the end of step 4.
TO USE: Thaw overnight at cool room temperature. On the hob, bring the lamb and sauce to the boil and simmer gently for 30 minutes. Complete as in steps 5-7.

Red Spiced Lamb

The meat should be well browned, so that the juices have a rich, dark colour. When serving, warn your guests to watch out for the whole spices.

Preparation time: 5 minutes
Cooking time: 2 hours 25 minutes
Cals per serving: 420
Serves 6

2.5 cm (1 inch) piece fresh root ginger	**2.5 cm (1 inch) stick cinnamon**
225 g (8 oz) onions	**5 ml (1 tsp) coriander seeds**
8 garlic cloves	**10 ml (2 tsp) cumin seeds**
1.1 kg (2½ lb) boned leg of lamb or stewing beef	**20 ml (4 tsp) paprika**
60 ml (4 tbsp) oil	**5 ml (1 tsp) cayenne pepper**
10 cardamom pods	**90 ml (6 tbsp) natural yogurt**
2 bay leaves	**600-750 ml (1-1¼ pints) lamb or beef stock**
6 whole cloves	**5 ml (1 tsp) salt**
10 peppercorns	

1 Peel and roughly chop the ginger and onions. Peel and crush the garlic. Pour 60 ml (4 tbsp) water into a blender or food processor. Add the ginger, garlic and onion and process until smooth. Cut the lamb into 4 cm (1½ inch) cubes.

2 Heat the oil in a large flameproof casserole and brown the meat in small batches; set aside. Add a little more oil if necessary and stir in the cardamom pods, bay leaves, cloves, peppercorns and cinnamon. Cook until the cloves begin to swell and the bay leaves to colour. Add the onion paste and cook for 4 minutes, stirring all the time, or until most of the liquid has evaporated.

3 Add the remaining spices, meat and juices and cook, stirring, for 1 minute. Add the yogurt, a spoonful at a time, cooking and stirring after each addition. Stir in just enough stock to cover the meat. Add the salt and bring to the boil.

4 Cover and cook at 180°C (350°F) Mark 4 for 1½-2 hours or until the meat is very tender. Spoon off any excess fat.

TO FREEZE: Cool, pack and freeze at the end of step 4.
TO USE: Thaw overnight at cool room temperature. Add 150 ml (¼ pint) lamb stock, bring to the boil, cover and reheat at 200°C (400°F) Mark 6 for 20-30 minutes.

Lamb and Lentil Bake

A spicy mix of minced lamb and lentils encased in filo pastry makes a warming and attractive-looking dish. Remember to keep the filo pastry covered with cling film whilst lining the tin, as filo dries out very quickly once exposed to the air and then becomes difficult to work with.

Preparation time: 20 minutes, plus cooling
Cooking time: 1¼ hours
Cals per serving: 520
Serves 4

125 g (4 oz) onion	**30 ml (2 tbsp) tomato purée**
2.5 cm (1 inch) piece fresh root ginger	**30 ml (2 tbsp) lemon juice**
30 ml (2 tbsp) oil	**50 g (2 oz) raisins**
1 garlic clove	**600 ml (1 pint) chicken stock**
2.5 ml (½ tsp) chilli seasoning	**salt and pepper**
2.5 ml (½ tsp) paprika	**50 g (2 oz) butter**
2.5 ml (½ tsp) dried marjoram	**about 125 g (4 oz) filo pastry**
225 g (8 oz) minced lamb or beef	**poppy seeds**
175 g (6 oz) red lentils	

1 Peel and finely chop the onion and ginger. Peel and crush the garlic. Heat the oil in a saucepan. Fry the onion for about 4-5 minutes until translucent. Stir in the ginger, garlic, chilli seasoning, paprika and marjoram. Cook, stirring for 1 minute. Add the mince and stir until it changes colour and is free of any lumps.

2 Mix in the lentils, tomato purée, lemon juice, raisins and stock. Cover and cook over a low heat for 20-25 minutes or until the lentils and mince are tender and most of the liquid is absorbed. Uncover and bubble off any excess liquid, stirring occasionally. Adjust seasoning then turn into a bowl and cool completely.

3 Melt the butter and lightly grease a 23 cm (9 inch) base measurement, 3 cm (1¼ inch) deep, loose-based fluted flan tin. Line with sheets of filo pastry, brushing with butter between the layers and overlapping them in a random manner. There should be no gaps in the pastry and the excess pastry should hang over the sides of the tin.

4 Spoon the cold filling into the flan case. Wrap over the pastry to enclose the filling. Brush with butter and garnish with crumpled up pastry trimmings. Brush with butter again. Sprinkle with poppy seeds.

5 Cook at 190°C (375°F) Mark 5 for about 50-55 minutes, covering lightly with foil after about 30-35 minutes. Cool for about 10 minutes before serving.

TO FREEZE: Pack and freeze at the end of step 4.
TO USE: Thaw overnight at cool room temperature. Cook as in step 5.

Navarin of Lamb with Spring Vegetables

A delicious lamb casserole, with glazed spring vegetables stirred in a the last moment.

Preparation time: 40 minutes
Cooking time: 1½ hours
Cals per serving: 425
Serves 6

900 g (2 lb) boned shoulder of lamb	**fresh thyme sprigs**
125 g (4 oz) each onion, carrot and celery	**2 bay leaves**
2 garlic cloves	**salt and pepper**
45 ml (3 tbsp) olive oil	**125 g (4 oz) each baby carrots, baby turnips and French beans**
15 ml (1 tbsp) plain flour	**175 g (6 oz) new potatoes**
30 ml (2 tbsp) tomato purée	**15 ml (1 tbsp) caster sugar**
150 ml (¼ pint) dry white wine	**25 g (1 oz) butter**
1 litre (1¾ pints) stock	**125 g (4 oz) asparagus**

1 Cut the lamb into 5 cm (2 inch) cubes. Peel and chop the onion, garlic and carrot. Chop celery.

2 Heat the oil in a large, flameproof casserole. Fry the lamb in batches over a high heat until well browned: remove with a slotted spoon. Add the onion, carrot and celery to the casserole and cook, stirring, for 10 minutes until soft and beginning to colour. Add the garlic with the flour and tomato purée. Cook for a further 2 minutes. Add the wine, bring to the boil and bubble to reduce by half. Add the lamb, stock, 3 thyme sprigs and bay leaves. Bring to the boil, stirring. Cover and cook at 150°C (300°F) Mark 2 for 1 hour.

3 Remove the lamb and thyme from the casserole, then purée vegetables with the stock in a food processor. Return to the casserole with the lamb and simmer for 5 minutes. If the sauce is too thick, add water; season.

4 Trim the carrots, turnips and beans. Place the carrots, turnips and potatoes in a frying pan with the sugar, butter and 300 ml (½ pint) water. Bring to the boil, then simmer for 15 minutes or until the water has evaporated and the vegetables are tender and glazed.

5 Meanwhile, bring a pan of salted water to the boil. Cook the beans for 2 minutes, then add the asparagus. Cook for a further 3 minutes, drain and stir into the lamb with the glazed vegetables.

TO FREEZE: Complete to end of step 3. Cool, pack and freeze.

TO USE: Thaw overnight at cool room temperature. Add 150 ml (¼ pint) stock, bring to the boil, cover and reheat at 180°C (350°F) Mark 4 for 35-40 minutes.

Shepherd's Pie

Celeriac is added to the topping, giving a twist to this classic family fare.

Preparation time: 20 minutes
Cooking time: 1½ hours
Cals per serving: 760
Serves 4

700 g (1½ lb) onions	**100 ml (4 fl oz) beef stock**
2 garlic cloves	**10 ml (2 tsp) lemon juice**
45 ml (3 tbsp) oil	**salt and pepper**
5 ml (1 tsp) caster sugar	**700 g (1½ lb) potatoes**
10 ml (2 tsp) paprika	**700 g (1½ lb) celeriac**
450 g (1 lb) minced lamb	**1 egg yolk**
30 ml (2 tbsp) plain white flour	**25 g (1 oz) butter**
400 g (14 oz) can chopped tomatoes	**50 g (2 oz) Lancashire cheese**
15 ml (1 tbsp) tomato purée	

1 Peel and chop the onions. Peel and crush the garlic. Heat the oil in a saucepan and fry the onions with the garlic and sugar for 10 minutes or until well browned.

2 Add the paprika and lamb: cook until browned, stirring often. Stir in the flour, tomatoes, tomato purée, stock, lemon juice and salt and pepper. Bring to the boil, cover and simmer for 30-40 minutes or until tender. Skim.

3 Meanwhile, peel and chop the potatoes and celeriac. Cook together in boiling, salted water for 20 minutes or until tender. Drain. Mash, then stir in the yolk, butter and seasoning.

4 Pour the hot lamb into a 1.7 litre (3 pint) shallow ovenproof dish. Spoon the potato mixture over and sprinkle with finely grated cheese.

5 Bake at 200°C (400°F) Mark 6 for 40 minutes or until piping hot and golden brown.

TO FREEZE: Cool, pack and freeze at the end of step 4.
TO USE: Thaw overnight at cool room temperature. Cook as in step 5 for 50 minutes or until piping hot.

Pork Hotpot

A warming dish of pork and beans, ideal to serve with baked potatoes on a chilly night.

Preparation time: 20 minutes, plus marinating
Cooking time: 2 hours
Cals per serving: 685
Serves 8

1.4 kg (3 lb) boned shoulder of pork	**450 g (1 lb) onions**
6 garlic cloves	**30 ml (2 tbsp) tomato purée**
105 ml (7 tbsp) oil	**two 400 g (14 oz) cans haricot or flageolet beans**
30 ml (2 tbsp) red wine vinegar	**two 400 g (14 oz) cans chopped tomatoes**
60 ml (4 tbsp) soft brown sugar	**300 ml (½ pint) red wine**
10 ml (2 tsp) minced chilli or few drops chilli sauce	**4 bay leaves**
salt and pepper	**25 g (1 oz) butter**
15 ml (3 tsp) dried oregano	**125 g (4 oz) white breadcrumbs, from French bread or ciabatta**
10 ml (2 tsp) dried thyme	**125 g (4 oz) grated Gruyère cheese**

1 Cut the pork into 2.5 cm (1 inch) cubes. Peel and crush the garlic. Place the pork in a large bowl with the garlic, 30 ml (2 tbsp) oil, vinegar, sugar, chilli, salt, pepper and 10 ml (2 tsp) oregano and all the thyme. Mix well, cover and leave in the refrigerator for at least 8 hours.

2 Peel, halve and slice the onions. Drain the pork, reserving the marinade.

3 Heat 45 ml (3 tbsp) oil in a large flameproof casserole and fry the pork in batches until well browned and sealed on all sides. Set aside. Add the remaining oil with the onions and cook for 10 minutes over a high heat, stirring occasionally, until they are soft and caramelised. Add the tomato purée and cook for 1 minute. Return the meat to the casserole with the drained bean juice, tomatoes, wine, bay leaves and the reserved marinade. Bring to the boil, stirring, cover and cook at 180°C (350°F) Mark 4 for 2 hours until pork is very tender.

4 About 20 minutes before the end of the cooking time, stir in the beans.

5 Turn up the oven to 200°C (400°F) Mark 6 and move the pork to a lower shelf. Melt the butter in a roasting tin, add the breadcrumbs, the remaining oregano and season with salt and pepper. Brown on the top shelf for 10 minutes. Serve the hotpot sprinkled with the crumbs and the cheese.

TO FREEZE: Complete to the end of step 4. Cool quickly, pack and freeze.

TO USE: Thaw overnight at cool room temperature. Add 150 ml (¼ pint) stock and bring to the boil. Cover and reheat at 180°C (350°F) Mark 4 for 25 minutes, then complete as in step 5.

Mustard Pork with Tomatoes

Cherry tomatoes and grainy mustard add the final delicious touch to this succulent, sherry-flavoured pork and mushroom dish. Serve with mixed roasted root vegetables.

Preparation time: 30 minutes, plus marinating
Cooking time: 1¼ hours
Cals per serving: 580
Serves 4

450 g (1 lb) onions	**10 ml (2 tsp) plain flour**
750 g (1½ lb) boned shoulder or pork, trimmed	**450 ml (68**
90 ml (6 tbsp) oil	**¾ pint) chicken stock**
10 ml (2 tsp) chopped fresh rosemary	**10 ml (2 tsp) dark soy sauce**
25 g (1 oz) butter	**salt and pepper**
3 garlic cloves	**450 g (1 lb) small, dark, flat mushrooms**
60 ml (4 tbsp) tomato purée	**45 ml (3 tbsp) grainy mustard**
100 ml (4 fl oz) dry sherry	

1 Peel and quarter the onions. Cut the pork into 2.5 cm (1 inch) chunks. Mix the pork with 30 ml (2 tbsp) oil and the rosemary; cover and set aside in a cool place for 2 hours.

2 Heat the butter in a flameproof casserole until just beginning to colour. Add the pork in batches and fry to a rich golden brown. Remove and set aside.

3 Lower the heat and add the onions. Cook for 5-7 minutes or until softened and golden. Peel and crush the garlic and add to the onions with the tomato purée. Fry for 2-3 minutes. Pour in the dry sherry and bring to the boil. Bubble to reduce by half.

4 Blend in the flour, stirring until smooth, then pour in the stock. Bring to the boil; return the pork to the pan with the soy sauce and season with salt and pepper. Simmer for 5 minutes, cover tightly and cook at 180°C (350°F) Mark 4 for 1-1¼ hours, until tender.

5 Meanwhile, heat the remaining oil in a large frying pan, add the mushrooms and fry briskly for 3-4 minutes. Season and add to the casserole 10 minutes before the end of the cooking time.

6 Stir in the mustard, return to the boil and add the tomatoes. Heat through for 1-2 minutes, then serve.

TO FREEZE: Complete to the end of step 5. Cool quickly, pack and freeze.
TO USE: Thaw overnight at cool room temperature. Place the pork mixture in a flameproof casserole, cover and bring to the boil over a gentle heat. Add the grainy mustard and reheat at 180°C (350°F) Mark 4 for 25-30 minutes or until hot through. Add the cherry tomatoes, leave to stand for 5 minutes, then serve.

Harvest Pork Casserole

Pork and apples form a natural partnership. Here they are combined with parsnips, onions and spices to create a dish with a distinctly autumnal feel.

Preparation time: 20 minutes
Cooking time: 1½ hours
Cals per serving: 530-355
Serves 4-6

700 g (1½ lb) boneless leg of pork	**30 ml (2 tbsp) plain white flour**
225 g (8 oz) onions	**300 ml (½ pint) beef stock**
1 garlic clove	**300 ml (½ pint) apple juice or cider**
450 g (1 lb) parsnips	**salt and pepper**
oil	**2 small, crisp, red eating apples**
15 ml (1 tbsp) ground coriander	**TO GARNISH**
5 ml (1 tsp) cumin seeds or 15 ml (1 tbsp) ground cumin	**snipped chives**

1 Cut the pork into bite-sized pieces. Peel and chop the onions; peel and crush the garlic; peel, halve and slice the parsnips.

2 Heat 45 ml (5 tbsp) oil in a flameproof casserole. Brown the meat well, then remove with a slotted spoon and drain on kitchen paper.

3 Sauté the onion and crushed garlic for 2-3 minutes. Add the parsnips, coriander and cumin and sauté for 2 minutes. Stir in the flour. Off the heat, gradually add the stock, apple juice and salt and pepper.

4 Bring the the boil and replace the meat. Cover and cook at 170°C (325°F) Mark 3 for 1¼ hours or until the pork is almost tender.

5 Quarter and roughly chop the apples. Stir them into the pork, cover and cook for a further 15-20 minutes or until tender. Season and garnish with snipped chives.

TO FREEZE: Cool, cover and freeze at the end of step 4.
TO USE: Thaw overnight at cool room temperature. Bring to the boil and complete as in step 5.

Peppered Pork Rounds

Lightly spiced pork and bacon patties make an unusual and tasty alternative to beef burgers.
Serve with a vegetable risotto to make a nourishing complete meal.

Preparation time: 20 minutes
Cooking time: 6 minutes
Cals per serving: 385
Serves 4

250 g (9 oz) shoulder of pork	**5 ml (1 tsp) coarsely ground black pepper**
250 g (9 oz) piece of rindless gammon	**2 garlic cloves**
125 g (4 oz) streaky bacon	**30 ml (2 tbsp) oil**
dash of chilli sauce	**TO GARNISH**
2.5 ml (½ tsp) dried thyme	**flat-leaf parsley**
2.5 ml (½ tsp) caster sugar	

1 Trim the pork and gammon of any excess fat. Roughly chop the pork, gammon and streaky bacon.

2 In a food processor, blend all the ingredients except the oil and parsley for about 1 minute or until quite smooth.

3 With wet hands, shape the mixture into 8 round, flat patties measuring about 9 cm (3½ inches) across.

4 Heat the oil in a large, non-stick frying pan. Fry the round patties in two batches for about 3 minutes on each side, or until golden brown and cooked through. Garnish with flat-leaf parsley and serve.

TO FREEZE: Prepare to the end of step 3. Place between two layers of greaseproof paper. Pack and freeze.
TO USE: Thaw overnight at cool room temperature and complete as in step 4.

Pork Fillets with Figs and Taleggio Cream

If you forget to soak the figs overnight, place them in a small saucepan with the wine and rosemary. Bring to the boil, cover and leave to soak for 20 minutes.

Preparation time: 20 minutes
Cooking time: about 40 minutes
Cals per serving: 715
Serves 6

12 ready-to-eat figs	**225 g (8 oz) Taleggio, Fontina, Delice de Bourgogne or Vignotte cheese**
100 ml (4 fl oz) white wine	**about 75 g (3 oz) Parma ham, sliced**
2 large sprigs fresh rosemary	**30 ml (2 tbsp) olive oil**
2 pork fillets	**25 g (1 oz) butter**
salt and pepper	**300 ml (½ pint) double cream**

1 Soak the figs overnight in the wine with one sprig of rosemary.

2 Drain the figs, reserving the wine, and remove the hard stalk from each fig. Split both pork fillets open lengthways like a book, cover with cling film and beat with a rolling pin until double their original width. Season with salt and pepper. Cut 25 g (1 oz) of the cheese into 12 small dice, then push a piece of cheese into each fig. Place the slices of Parma ham down the centre of each fillet, arrange the figs on top and fold over the Parma ham. Reshape the fillets, tying at intervals with fine string.

3 Sit the pork on the remaining rosemary sprig in a roasting tin, just large enough to hold them, and drizzle over the oil. Pour in the reserved wine.

4 Roast the pork at 200°C (400°F) Mark 6 for 30-35 minutes or until just tender.

5 Meanwhile, chop the remaining cheese and place in a saucepan with the butter. Pour in the cream and melt over a low heat until blended. Season lightly.

6 Spoon or brush a little of the cheese sauce over the pork for the last 15 minutes of cooking time. Cover the remainder and keep warm just off the heat.

7 Transfer the cooked fillets to a board and cover with foil. Scrape down the sediment from the sides of the roasting tin, and bring the pan juices to the boil. Bubble for 3-4 minutes until only 45-60 ml (3-4 tbsp) liquid remains. Stir into the remaining cheese sauce. Serve the sauce with the thickly sliced pork.

TO FREEZE: Prepare the pork to the end of step 2. Wrap and freeze. Cool, pack and freeze the cheese sauce.
TO USE: Thaw both the pork and sauce overnight in the refrigerator. Complete as in recipe.

Spicy Sausage and Chicken Liver Sauce

The coarse, spicy sausages used in this recipe are found in good delicatessens and have a firmer texture than traditional pork sausages. Or you could replace them with 75 g (3 oz) chopped coarse salami, stirring this in just before serving.

Preparation time: 10 minutes
Cooking time: about 35 minutes
Cals per serving: 800
Serves 4

225 g (8 oz) coarse spicy pork sausages	**150 ml (¼ pint) dry white wine**
125 g (4 oz) onion	**salt and pepper**
350 g (12 oz) chicken livers	**45 ml (3 tbsp) chopped fresh parsley**
45 ml (3 tbsp) olive oil	**TO SERVE**
25 g (1 oz) butter	**350 g (12 oz) pasta**
300 ml (½ pint) tomato passata	**freshly grated Parmesan cheese**

1 Skin the sausages and roughly crumble the meat. Peel and chop the onion. Trim and halve the livers.

2 Heat the oil and butter in a frying pan. Brown the chicken livers and remove with a slotted spoon. Stir in the onion and cook until softened.

3 Add the sausage meat and cook over a high heat until well browned, stirring well.

4 Stir in the passata and wine and bring to the boil. cover and simmer for 10-15 minutes. Add the chicken livers, cover and cook for 10 minutes.

5 Season with salt and pepper and stir in the chopped fresh parsley. Spoon over hot pasta tossed in grated Parmesan cheese.

TO FREEZE: Cool, pack and freeze at the end of step 4.
TO USE: Thaw overnight at cool room temperature. Reheat and stir in the parsley to serve.

Cheese and Ham Pie

This is a delicious mix of cheese; spinach and ham. For a vegetarian alternative replace the cooked ham with 225 g (8 oz) sliced brown-cap mushrooms which have been fried in butter until golden. Allow to cool before mixing with the cheese.

Preparation time: 30 minutes
Cooking time: 1¼ hours
Cals per serving: 565
Serves 6

450 g (about 1 lb) puff pastry	**salt and pepper**
275 g (10 oz) onions	**ground nutmeg**
25 g (1 oz) butter	**175 g (6 oz) Roquefort, Bleu D'Avergne or Stilton cheese**
2.5 ml (½ tsp) dried rosemary	
60 ml (4 tbsp) crème fraîche	**175 g (6 oz) sliced cooked ham**
450 g (1 lb) frozen leaf spinach	**beaten egg, to glaze**

1 Roll out half of the pastry to approximately 30.5 cm (12 inches) square. Place on a baking sheet, prick well all over and bake at 200°C (400°F) Mark 6 for about 12 minutes or until it is golden and crisp. Using a 25.5 cm (10 inch) dinner plate as a template, cut a round of cooked pastry. Set aside on the baking sheet.

2 Peel and finely chop the onions and fry gently in the butter and rosemary for a good 10-12 minutes or until very soft. Stir in the crème fraîche, remove from the heat and cool.

3 While the onions are cooking, squeeze all the excess liquid from the spinach and stir over a low heat until it is completely dry. Roughly chop. Season with salt, pepper and ground nutmeg.

4 Roll out all of the remaining pastry to a round that is about 30.5 cm (12 inches) in diameter.

5 Spread the cooled spinach over the cooked pastry round. Top with the onions, then the crumbled cheese. Finish with a layer of the sliced cooked ham. Lay the raw pastry over the top. Trim the excess pastry, leaving just enough to tuck neatly under the round.

6 Brush with beaten egg and cook at 200°C (400°F) Mark 6 for 40-45 minutes or until well risen and deep golden. Cover, if necessary.

TO FREEZE: Complete to the end of Step 5. Pack and freeze.

TO USE: Thaw overnight at cool room temperature. Cook as in step 6.

Braised Ham with Cherries

The rich, fruity flavour of the cherry sauce also goes well with roast duck or pork.

Preparation time: 10 minutes
Cooking time: 2½ hours
Cals per serving: 555
Serves 6

2 large celery sticks	**200 ml (7 fl oz) dry sherry**
150 g (5 oz) carrots	**900 ml (1½ pints) chicken stock**
250 g (9 oz) onions	**bouquet garni**
50 g (2 oz) dried cherries	**60 ml (4 tbsp) golden syrup**
50 g (2 oz) blanched almonds	**125 g (4 oz) pitted fresh or frozen cherries**
1 kg (2¼ lb) unsmoked gammon joint	**5 ml (1 tsp) cornflour**
30 ml (2 tbsp) oil	**lemon juice**

1 Roughly chop the celery. Peel and chop the carrots and onions. Pour 150 ml (¼ pint) boiling water over the dried cherries, leave to soak. Roughly chop almonds.

2 Place the gammon in a large saucepan, cover with cold water and bring to the boil slowly. Simmer gently for 30 minutes. Lift out the gammon; cool a little.

3 Meanwhile, heat the oil in a flameproof casserole, add the celery, carrots and onions, then cover and cook gently for 10 minutes. Add 100 ml (4 fl oz) sherry and bring to the boil, then bubble to reduce by half.

4 Peel the skin and most of the fat from the gammon and place the joint on top of the vegetables. Pour round 300 ml (½ pint) stock, add the bouquet garni, then bubble for 2-3 minutes. Cover and cook at 180°C (350°F) Mark 4 for 1-1¼ hours or until tender.

5 Drain the gammon, reserving the cooking liquid. Return the gammon to the wiped-out casserole and drizzle with 15 ml (1 tbsp) golden syrup. Sprinkle with the almonds. Return the gammon to the oven and cook at

200°C (400°F) Mark 6 for a further 15 minutes or until golden and glazed.

6 Place the remaining golden syrup in a saucepan and heat until a deep caramel colour. Add the remaining sherry and the soaking liquid from the dried cherries. Bubble to reduce by half. Pour on the reserved cooking liquid and the remaining stock. Bring to the boil and bubble for 15 minutes or until reduced by a third. Add all the cherries for the last 5 minutes.

7 Mix the cornflour with a little cold water, add to the sauce and return to boil, stirring until lightly thickened. Add lemon juice to taste. Serve hot with the gammon.

TO FREEZE: Slice the ham thinly and arrange the slices, overlapping, on a sheet of foil. Wrap up tightly as a flat parcel and freeze. Cool pack and freeze sauce.
TO USE: Thaw at cool room temperature overnight. Place the foil-wrapped ham in a roasting tin. Reheat at 200°C (400°F) Mark 6 for 25-35 minutes. Reheat the sauce.

Peppered Winter Stew

This peppery winter casserole is a total meal in itself, with meat and root vegetables cooked in one dish – a warming dish for cold winter days.

Preparation time: 30 minutes
Cooking time: 2 hours 20 minutes
Cals per serving: 425
Serves 6

225 g (8 oz) onions	**75 cl bottle red wine**
225 g (8 oz) shallots	**30 ml (2 tbsp) redcurrant jelly**
4 garlic cloves	**1 small bunch thyme**
900 g (2 lb) stewing venison, beef or lamb	**4 bay leaves**
salt and pepper	**15 ml (1 tbsp) coarsely ground black pepper**
25 g (1 oz) plain flour	**6 cloves**
75 ml (5 tbsp) oil	**600-900 ml (1½ pints) beef stock**
30 ml (2 tbsp) tomato purée	**900 g (2 lb) mixed root vegetables, such as carrots, parsnips, turnips and celeriac**
100 ml (4 fl oz) red wine vinegar	

1 Peel and finely chop the onions. Peel the shallots, leaving the root end intact to keep them whole while cooking. Peel and crush the garlic. Cut the meat into 4 cm (1½ inch) cubes and toss in the seasoned flour.

2 Heat 45 ml (3 tbsp) oil in a large, deep flameproof casserole and brown the meat well in small batches. Remove and set aside. Wipe out the pan, heat the remaining oil and fry the shallots for 4-5 minutes or until golden. Remove with a slotted spoon and set aside.

3 Add the chopped onions and crushed garlic to the pan, cook, stirring, for 5-7 minutes or until soft and golden. Add the tomato purée and cook for a further 2 minutes. Add the vinegar and wine and bring to the boil. Bubble for 10 minutes.

4 Add the redcurrant jelly, thyme, bay leaves, pepper, cloves and meat to the pan. Add enough stock to barely cover the meat then bring to the boil, cover and cook at 180°C (350°F) Mark 4 for 1-1½ hours or until the meat is very tender.

5 Meanwhile peel and cut the root vegetables into 4 cm (1½ inch) chunks.

6 Remove the meat from the casserole and reserve. Strain the liquid through a fine sieve, pushing through the residue. Return the liquid with the meat, vegetables and browned shallots, to the casserole. Bring to the boil, cover and return to the oven for a further 45-50 minutes or until the vegetables are tender.

TO FREEZE: Cool, pack and freeze at the end of step 6.
TO USE: Thaw overnight at cool room temperature. Add an extra 150 ml (¼ pint) stock. Bring slowly to the boil. Cover and reheat at 180°C (350°F) Mark 4 for 30 minutes.

VEGETABLE DISHES

Mushroom and Roasted Potato Bake

A delicious all-in-one vegetarian dish, serve with baked tomatoes for a flavourful meat-free meal.

Preparation time: 45 minutes
Cooking time: 35 minutes
Cals per serving: 795
Serves 6

900 g (2 lb) small potatoes	25 g (1 oz) dried porcini mushrooms (optional)
90 ml (6 tbsp) olive oil	10 ml (2 tsp) chopped fresh thyme
225 g (8 oz) onions	300 ml (½ pint) each white wine and vegetable stock
2 garlic cloves	300 ml (½ pint) double cream
225 g (8 oz) mixed mushrooms, such as shiitake and brown cap	125 g (4 oz) freshly grated Parmesan cheese
400 g (14 oz) large fresh spinach leaves	salt and pepper
175 g (6 oz) Gruyère cheese	300 ml (½ pint) Greek yogurt
30 ml (2 tbsp) tomato purée	2 eggs
60 ml (4 tbsp) sun-dried tomato paste	

1 Wash and quarter the potatoes. Toss with 60 ml (4 tbsp) oil in a large roasting tin. Cook at 200°C (400°F) Mark 6 for 40 minutes or until tender and golden. Peel and roughly chop the onions. Peel and crush the garlic. Roughly chop the mushrooms and spinach. Grate the Gruyère cheese.

2 Heat the remaining oil in a large, heavy-based saucepan. Add the onion and cook for 10 minutes or until soft, then add the garlic and mushrooms and cook over a high heat for 5 minutes. Stir in the tomato pastes, porcini mushrooms, if using, and the thyme and wine. Bring to the boil and simmer for 2 minutes.

3 Add the stock and cream, bring back to the boil and bubble for 20 minutes or until well reduced and syrupy. Pour into a 2.3 litre (4 pint) ovenproof dish. Stir in the potatoes, spinach, Gruyère and half the Parmesan cheese. Season well with salt and pepper.

4 Combine the yogurt with the beaten eggs and season. Spoon over the vegetable mixture and sprinkle with the remaining Parmesan cheese.

5 Cook at 200°C (400°F) Mark 6 for 30-35 minutes or until golden and bubbling.

TO FREEZE: Cool, pack and freeze at the end of step 4.
TO USE: Thaw overnight at cool room temperature, then cook as in step 5 for 40-45 minutes or until golden.

Mixed Bean Chilli

Serve this vegetarian version of the popular Mexican chilli with tortillas or rice.

Preparation time: 20 minutes, plus soaking
Cooking time: About 2½-3 hours
Cals per serving: 275
Serves 6

125 g (4 oz) dried red kidney beans	**15 ml (1 tbsp) tomato purée**
125 g (4 oz) dried black-eye beans	**10 ml (2 tsp) cumin seeds**
salt and pepper	**2 bay leaves**
1 red onion	**1 cinnamon stick**
3 garlic cloves	**425 g (15 oz) can chopped tomatoes**
2 dried hot red chillies	**15 ml (1 tbsp) lime or lemon juice**
700 g (1½ lb) mixed vegetables, such as carrots, potatoes, peppers, aubergines	**large handful of fresh coriander**
60 ml (4 tbsp) olive oil	**TO SERVE**
15 ml (1 tbsp) mild paprika	**soured cream**
	grated Manchego or Cheddar cheese

1 Put the dried beans in separate bowls and pour on enough cold water to cover. Leave to soak overnight.

2 Drain the beans and put them in separate pans with enough water to cover. Boil each rapidly for 10 minutes, then simmer the red kidney beans for 1-1½ hours and the black-eye beans for 1½ hours until tender. Add salt towards the end of the cooking time. Drain and rinse.

3 Peel and finely chop the onion. Peel and crush the garlic. Crumble the chillies. Prepare the vegetables, cutting them into fairly large chunks.

4 Heat half the oil in a large pan. Add the onion, half of the garlic and the chillies. Cook, stirring, for 5 minutes or until the onion is softened. Add the paprika, tomato purée and cumin seeds and cook, stirring, for 2 minutes. Add the bay leaves and cinnamon stick.

5 Add the beans and prepared vegetables. Cook for 2 minutes, then add the tomatoes and 150 ml (¼ pint) water. Bring to the boil, lower the heat and simmer for about ¾-1 hour until the vegetables are tender.

6 Meanwhile, whisk together the rest of the oil, lime or lemon juice and garlic. Roughly chop the remaining coriander and stir into the oil mixture. Leave to stand.

7 When the chilli is cooked, stir in the coriander mixture. Check the seasoning if necessary. Serve topped with soured cream and grated cheese.

TO FREEZE: Cool, pack and freeze at the end of step 5.
TO USE: Thaw overnight at cool room temperature and reheat until piping hot. Complete the recipe.

Crusty Mediterranean Parcels

Plaited pastry parcels, encasing Mediterranean vegetables, make a good vegetarian party dish.

Preparation time: 30 minutes
Cooking time: 1 hour 10 minutes
Cals per serving: 480
Serves 8

700 g (1½ lb) mixed vegetables, such as carrots, leeks, courgettes, red peppers, aubergines	**125 g (4 oz) Gruyère cheese**
30 ml (2 tbsp) olive oil	**200 g (7 oz) mascarpone cheese**
salt and pepper	**50 ml (2 fl oz) single cream**
225 g (8 oz) onions	**30 ml (2 tbsp) finely chopped fresh chives**
2 garlic cloves	**50 g (2 oz) pine nuts, toasted**
400 g (14 oz) can chopped tomatoes	**450 g (1 lb) packet puff pastry**
15 ml (1 tbsp) sun-dried tomato paste	**1 egg**

1 Chop the vegetables into 2.5 cm (1 inch) chunks. Place in a small roasting tin with 15 ml (1 tbsp) olive oil and season with salt and pepper. Cook at 200°C (400°F) Mark 6 for 40-45 minutes or until just tender, stirring occasionally. Remove from the oven. Cool.

2 Peel and roughly chop the onions. Peel and crush the garlic. Heat the remaining olive oil in a frying pan. Add the onions and crushed garlic and fry for 5 minutes or until lightly coloured. Add the chopped tomatoes and tomato paste and simmer, uncovered, for 15-20 minutes or until thick and pulpy. Set aside.

3 Grate the Gruyère cheese. Mix 75 g (3 oz) with the mascarpone cheese, single cream and chopped chives. Mix the vegetables with the tomato sauce, 25 g (1 oz) pine nuts and seasoning. Roll out the pastry quite thinly to 2 rectangles measuring about 35.5 x 30.5 cm (14 x 12 inches).

4 Beat the egg with a pinch of salt. Place half the vegetables down the centre of each oblong, about 10 cm (4 inches) wide. Top the vegetables with the cheese mixture. Brush the pastry with the egg glaze.

5 With a sharp knife, make diagonal incisions about 2.5 cm (1 inch) apart, down each side of the filling to within 2.5 cm (1 inch) of the filling. Plait from the top by overlapping alternate strips from either side across the filling. Make sure that the strips cross over or the pastry may burst in cooking. Tuck any loose pastry under the base. Brush liberally with egg glaze and sprinkle with pepper, coarse salt, remaining cheese and pine nuts.

6 Place the plaits on a baking sheet. Cook at 220°C (425°F) Mark 7 for 25 minutes or until golden. Cover loosely with foil if they begin to brown too quickly.

TO FREEZE: Open-freeze and wrap at the end of step 5.
TO USE: Thaw for 4 hours at room temperature; cook as in step 6 for 35 minutes or until golden brown and hot.

Courgette and Thyme Tart

The pastry case for this flan is baked blind with an egg glaze to ensure a really crisp texture. The fresh-tasting filling makes the dish ideal for a light supper or lunch.

Preparation time: 45 minutes, plus chilling
Cooking time: 1 hour 10 minutes
Cals per serving: 620
Serves 6

125 g (4 oz) chilled butter	**30 ml (2 tbsp) olive oil**
125 g (4 oz) plain flour	**salt and pepper**
pinch of salt	**15 ml (1 tbsp) small sprigs of thyme**
350 g (12 oz) courgettes	**300 g (11 oz) medium-fat soft goats' cheese**
1 bunch spring onions	**3 eggs**
125 g (4 oz) feta cheese	**200 ml (7 fl oz) double cream**

1 To make the pastry, cut the butter into small cubes. Place in a food processor with the flour and salt. Process for 2-3 seconds, then add 60 ml (4 tbsp) cold water. Process for 3-4 seconds or until the mixture just comes together in a ball. Turn out on to a floured work surface and knead lightly until the ball of dough has a smooth surface but the butter is still in small pieces. Wrap and chill for at least 2 hours.

2 Roughly chop the courgettes. Slice the spring onions and crumble the feta cheese into large pieces.

3 In a large frying pan, heat the olive oil, add the spring onions and cook for 1-2 minutes. Add the courgettes and cook for a further 2-3 minutes. Season with salt and pepper and add the thyme. Turn into a wide bowl to cool.

4 In a large bowl, combine the goats' cheese, 2 eggs, cream, feta cheese and the cooled courgettes. Set aside in a cool place.

5 On a lightly floured surface, roll the pastry out thinly and line a 23 cm (9 inch) loose-bottom flan tin; chill for 20 minutes.

6 Line with greaseproof paper and fill with baking beans. Cook at 200°C (400°F) Mark 6 for 15 minutes, remove the paper and baking beans and cook for a further 10-15 minutes or until a deep russet brown. Allow to cool for 5 minutes, brush the inside of the pastry case with the remaining beaten egg and return it to the oven for 4-5 minutes or until the egg has formed a seal. Pour in the courgette and cheese mixture and cook for 30-35 minutes or until the filling is just set.

7 Leave the tart to cool for 5 minutes, then carefully unmould it on to a cooling rack. Serve warm or cold.

TO FREEZE: Complete to the end of step 6, cool quickly on a cooling rack, wrap and freeze.

TO USE: Place the frozen tart on a preheated baking sheet and cook at 200°C (400°F) Mark 6 for 50 minutes. (It may be necessary to cover the tart with a tent of foil to prevent over-browning.)

Roasted Vegetable and Pasta Gratin

Aubergines, peppers and squash are roasted to bring out their delicious flavour, then combined with pasta and spinach to create a satisfying dish. For variety, you can add cooked ham or chicken with the spinach.

Preparation time: 35 minutes
Cooking time: 1½ hours
Cals per serving: 585
Serves 8

700 g (1½ lb) mixed peppers	50 g (2 oz) butter
450 g (1 lb) aubergines	50 g (2 oz) plain flour
450 g (1 lb) squash, such as butternut or pumpkin, peeled	900 ml (1½ pints) milk
90 ml (6 tbsp) olive oil	30 ml (2 tbsp) wholegrain mustard
225 g (8 oz) dried pasta shapes	150 g (5 oz) soft cheese with garlic and herbs, such as Boursin
450 g (1 lb) frozen leaf spinach, thawed	salt and pepper
225 g (8 oz) mature Cheddar cheese	

1 Deseed the peppers and cut into bite-sized pieces. Cut the aubergines and squash into bite-sized pieces and put in two roasting tins with the oil. Roast at 220°C (425°F) Mark 7 for 45 minutes or until tender and charred.

2 Meanwhile, cook the pasta shapes and drain them thoroughly. Squeeze the excess liquid from the frozen spinach and grate the Cheddar cheese.

3 Melt the butter in a pan, and then stir in the flour. Cook, stirring, for 1 minute before adding the milk. Bring to the boil, stirring all the time. Simmer for 2-3 minutes or until the sauce thickens. Off the heat, add the mustard, soft cheese and all but 50 g (2 oz) of the Cheddar. Stir thoroughly until smooth. Season well with salt and pepper.

4 Mix the pasta, spinach and roasted vegetables with the sauce. Now spoon the vegetable and pasta gratin into a large, shallow ovenproof dish and sprinkle the remaining 50 g (2 oz) Cheddar cheese over the top.

5 Stand the dish on a baking sheet and cook at 200°C (400°F) Mark 6 for about 40 minutes or until hot and golden brown, covering with aluminium foil, if necessary, to prevent over browning.

TO FREEZE: Cool, pack and freeze at the end of step 4.
TO USE: Thaw overnight at a cool room temperature. Cook as in step 5 for about 1 hour.

Potato and Fennel Gratin

A good way of freezing potatoes, this gratin dish makes an excellent accompaniment to a meaty casserole. For a vegetarian meal, try serving the gratin with mixed, roasted Mediterranean vegetables.

Preparation time: 5 minutes
Cooking time: 1 hour
Cals per serving: 255
Serves 6

450 g (1 lb) fennel	**2 garlic cloves**
salt and pepper	**300 ml (½ pint) double cream**
700 g (1½ lb) large potatoes	**300 ml (½ pint) milk**

1 Trim the feathery leaves and stalks off the fennel. Halve and thinly slice. Cook the fennel in boiling, salted water for 2 minutes, drain, then set aside. Peel and thinly slice the potatoes. Peel and crush the garlic.

2 In a large saucepan bring the cream and milk to the boil with the garlic. Add the potatoes and fennel. Bring to the boil and simmer over a low heat. Cook for 15-20 minutes, stirring from time to time, to prevent the potatoes from sticking. Season well with salt and pepper and spoon the potato mixture into a 2 litre (3½ pint) ovenproof dish.

3 Cook at 200°C (400°F) Mark 6 for 40 minutes or until the gratin is golden and tender.

TO FREEZE: Cool, pack and freeze at the end of step 2.
TO USE: Thaw overnight at cool room temperature, then cook as in step 3.

Summer Vegetable Soufflé

A lovely, light dish, this soufflé makes the most of seasonal vegetables and is deliciously foolproof too.

Preparation time: 50 minutes, plus chilling/infusing

Cooking time: 1 hour

Cals per serving: 420

Serves 6

25 g (1 oz) Parmesan cheese	**salt and pepper**
50 g (2 oz) Gruyère cheese	**350 g (12 oz) spinach**
65 g (2½ oz) butter	**60 ml (4 tbsp) olive oil**
300 ml (½ pint) milk	**5 ml (1 tsp) chopped fresh thyme**
2 bay leaves	**2 garlic cloves, crushed**
4 peppercorns	**30 ml (2 tbsp) sun-dried tomato paste**
125 g (4 oz) each red peppers, onions, courgettes and aubergines	**100 ml (4 fl oz) white wine**
	50 g (2 oz) plain flour
175 g (6 oz) tomatoes	**6 eggs, separated**

1 Finely grate the Parmesan and Gruyère cheeses into 2 separate bowls. Tie a double band of greaseproof paper around a 1.7 litre (3 pint) soufflé dish to form a collar. Brush the inside of the dish and the collar with 15 g (½ oz) melted butter, then sprinkle with 30 ml (2 tbsp) of the grated Parmesan. Place the soufflé dish on a baking sheet and chill for 30 minutes. Put the milk, bay leaves and peppercorns in a small pan. Gently bring to the boil, then set aside to infuse for 30 minutes.

2 Meanwhile, deseed and finely dice the red pepper; peel and chop the onions; dice the courgettes and aubergines. Skin, deseed and finely dice the tomatoes. Bring a large pan of salted water to the boil, add the spinach and cook for 1 minute. Drain and refresh immediately in cold water to set the colour. Drain again, allow to cool. Squeeze well to remove excess water, then finely chop.

3 To make the ratatouille, heat the oil in a large non-stick frying pan and add the onions, thyme and garlic. Cook, stirring, for 10 minutes, or until the onions are soft and golden. Add the peppers, courgettes and aubergines and cook, stirring, over a high heat for 5 minutes. Stir in the sun-dried tomato paste, wine and diced tomatoes, bring to the boil and simmer for 15 minutes, or until most of the liquid has evaporated. Remove from the heat, season and set aside to cool.

4 Melt the remaining 50 g (2 oz) butter in a saucepan, stir in the flour and cook for 1 minute, stirring all the time. Remove the pan from the heat, gradually stir in the cooled, strained milk, then return to the heat and bring to the boil, stirring all the time, until the sauce has thickened. Beat in the chopped spinach; allow to cool. Add the egg yolks, along with both the grated cheeses, reserving 30 ml (2 tbsp). Season well with salt and black pepper.

5 Spoon the cooked ratatouille mixture into the prepared soufflé dish. In a mixing bowl, whisk the 6 egg whites with a pinch of salt until they reach soft peaks. Next, using a large metal spoon, stir a spoonful of the whisked egg whites into the cooled spinach and cheese mixture in order to lighten it. Fold in the remaining egg whites.

6 Spoon the spinach mixture into the soufflé dish to cover the ratatouille. Run a knife around the inside edge of the dish to ensure that the soufflé rises evenly, then sprinkle the reserved grated cheese on top and chill for up to 2 hours. Cook the soufflé at 190°C (375°F) Mark 5 for 55 minutes-1 hour, or until the soufflé is well risen and golden on top. Serve immediately.

TO FREEZE: Open-freeze and wrap the uncooked soufflé.
TO USE: Cook from frozen at 190°C (375°F) Mark 5 for 50 minutes.

Bubble and Squeak Cakes

Delicious served with a saucy meat dish, these tasty cabbage, leek and potato cakes reheat very successfully from frozen – a useful vegetable dish to have on standby.

Preparation time: 15 minutes
Cooking time: 45 minutes
Cals per serving: 260
Serves 6

175 g (6 oz) green cabbage		**125 g (4 oz) butter**
175 g (6 oz) leeks		**15 ml (1 tbsp) oil**
550 g (1¼ lb) old potatoes		**flour for dusting**
salt and pepper		

1 Finely shred the cabbage and leeks. Peel the potatoes, then cook in a large pan of boiling, salted water until tender. Drain and mash.

2 Melt 50 g (2 oz) of the butter in a large non-stick frying pan, add the leeks and cabbage and fry for 5 minutes, stirring, or until soft and beginning to colour. Combine the cabbage and leeks with the potatoes and season well.

3 When cool enough to handle, mould into 12 cakes and dust with flour.

4 Heat the oil and remaining butter in a non-stick frying pan and cook the cakes for 4 minutes on each side or until they are golden, crisp and hot through.

TO FREEZE: Cool, pack and freeze the cakes at the end of the recipe.
TO USE: Reheat from frozen at 220°C (425°F) Mark 7 for 25 minutes.

Coriander Rosti

A different way of serving potatoes, this rosti is guaranteed to add interest to any meal.
It's also easy to make – grated potato is flavoured with onion and fresh coriander, then baked
until appetisingly golden in colour.

Preparation time: 15 minutes
Cooking time: 1 hour 25 minutes
Cals per serving: 100
Serves 6

1.4 kg (3 lb) baking potatoes	**15 ml (1 tbsp) chopped fresh coriander**
225 g (8 oz) large onion	**salt and pepper**
40 g (1½ oz) butter	

1 Bake the potatoes at 200°C (400°F) Mark 6 for 40 minutes until slightly softened but not cooked through.

2 Peel and finely chop the onion. Heat the butter in a pan and sauté the onion until soft, about 5-7 minutes.

3 Leave the potatoes in the skins until cool, then peel and grate coarsely. Gently stir into the onion with the coriander. Season well with salt and pepper.

4 Grease a baking sheet. Divide the mixture into rough mounds and place on the baking sheet.

5 Bake at 200°C (400°F) Mark 6 for 40 minutes or until crisp and golden.

TO FREEZE: Open-freeze at the end of step 4 and cover.
TO USE: Cook from frozen at 200°C (400°F) Mark 6 for 45 minutes.

Swede and Orange Purée

Root purées freeze well, making them a useful accompaniment. Here swede is given a lift with the addition of orange and soured cream – a mouthwatering combination of flavours.

Preparation time: 15 minutes
Cooking time: 30 minutes
Cals per serving: 100
Serves 4

1.1 kg (2½ lb) swede	**30 ml (2 tbsp) orange juice**
salt and pepper	**45 ml (3 tbsp) soured cream**
25 g (1 oz) butter or margarine	**TO GARNISH**
finely grated rind of 1 orange	**parsley**

1 Peel the swede and slice quite thinly. Put into a saucepan, cover with cold salted water and bring to the boil. Cook for about 20 minutes, until quite tender. Allow to drain thoroughly in a colander for several minutes.

2 Mash the swede, then add the butter, salt and pepper and grated orange rind. Stir over a moderate heat for several minutes until thoroughly hot and all excess moisture has been driven off.

3 Stir in the orange juice and the soured cream. Reheat gently, stirring all the time to prevent the purée sticking to the pan. Sprinkle with pepper and garnish with parsley.

TO FREEZE: Cool, pack and freeze at the end of step 2.
TO USE: Thaw overnight in the refrigerator, then gently reheat and complete step 3.

Dal with Ginger

An Indian pulse dish, perfect to serve with spicy grills, or as a fibre-rich addition to a vegetarian meal. Ginger, garlic, turmeric and chilli give the dish its spicy, aromatic character.

Preparation time: 10 minutes
Cooking time: about 50 minutes
Cals per serving: 190
Serves 6

---

225 g (8 oz) split black dal or urid dal (de-husked, split black dal) or split green lentils

125 g (4 oz) onion

25 g (1 oz) piece fresh root ginger

1 garlic clove

45 ml (3 tbsp) oil

5 ml (1 tsp) ground turmeric

2.5 ml (½ tsp) hot chilli powder

salt and pepper

---

1 Place the dal in a sieve and rinse well under cold water; drain well. Peel and roughly chop the onion; peel and finely chop the ginger; peel and crush the garlic.

2 Heat the oil in a heavy-based saucepan. Add the onion, ginger and garlic and fry for 3-4 minutes or until beginning to brown, stirring occasionally to prevent them from sticking.

3 Add the dal and spices and cook for 1 minute, stirring all the time. Pour in 750 ml (1¼ pints) water; season and bring to the boil.

4 Cover the pan and simmer for 40-45 minutes or until most of the liquid is absorbed and dal is tender. Stir occasionally and check the liquid level as dals have different rates of absorption. If the dal seems to be getting very dry, add a little more water. If the dal is tender with a lot of excess liquid, uncover the pan and bubble off the liquid. Adjust the seasoning and serve.

TO FREEZE: Cool, pack and freeze at the end of the recipe.
TO USE: Thaw overnight at cool room temperature, place in a greased ovenproof dish and reheat at 180°C (350°F) Mark 4 for about 1 hour. Stir thoroughly before serving – the dal will become slightly mushier after freezing.

DESSERTS

Apricot and Banana Mascarpone Tart

An easy-to-make pastry case, filled with a luscious combination of fresh fruit and creamy cheese, this dessert makes an irresistible finale to any meal.

Preparation time: 20 minutes, plus chilling

Cooking time: 35 minutes

Cals per serving: 410

Serves 8

175 g (6 oz) plain white flour	**2 eggs**
75 g (3 oz) caster sugar	**1.25 ml (¼ tsp) vanilla essence**
75 g (3 oz) butter	**30 ml (2 tbsp) soft dark brown (muscovado) sugar**
350 g (12 oz) fresh apricots	**60 ml (4 tbsp) apricot jam**
1 banana	**TO SERVE**
225 g (8 oz) tub mascarpone cheese or 200 g (7 oz) full-fat soft cheese blended with 150 ml (¼ pint) single cream	**single cream**

1 In a food processor, blend the flour and 50 g (2 oz) caster sugar. Add the butter and process until the mixture resembles breadcrumbs. Add 45-60 ml (3-4 tbsp) water and blend again until the mixture forms a rough dough. Turn out on to a work surface and gently knead until smooth. Wrap and chill for 30 minutes.

2 Roll out the dough and use to line a 34 x 11.5 cm (13½ x 4½ inch) loose-based, fluted tranche tin or a 23 cm (9 inch) flan tin. Chill the pastry case for 30 minutes, then line with greaseproof paper and baking beans. Bake at 200°C (400°F) Mark 6 for about 15 minutes or until just set. Remove baking beans and paper and return the pastry case to the oven for a further 15 minutes.

3 Halve and stone the apricots. Slice the banana. Spoon the fruit into the pastry case. Whisk together the next three ingredients with the remaining 25 g (1 oz) caster sugar until smooth. Spoon over the fruit and sprinkle with the muscovado sugar.

4 Bake at 170°C (325°F) Mark 3 for about 35 minutes or until just set.

5 Warm the jam in a saucepan until bubbling, then brush over the tart to glaze. Serve warm with cream.

TO FREEZE: Cool, pack and freeze at the end of step 4.
TO USE: Thaw at cool, room temperature for 4 hours. Cover loosely with foil and warm through in the oven at 180°C (350°F) Mark 4 for 15-20 minutes. Complete as in step 5.

Frangipane Baked Pears

Whole pears are poached, then baked in a delicious almond sponge mixture.

Preparation time: 15 minutes, plus soaking
Cooking time: 1 hour 20 minutes
Cals per serving: 575
Serves 6

25 g (1 oz) raisins	**6 pears**
25 g (1 oz) chopped almonds	**15 ml (1 tbsp) apricot jam**
25 g (1 oz) mixed peel	**125 g (4 oz) butter**
45 ml (3 tbsp) kirsch or rum	**2 eggs**
75 g (3 oz) flaked almonds	**few drops of almond essence (optional)**
50 g (2 oz) plain flour	**TO SERVE**
225 g (8 oz) caster sugar	**extra-thick cream**

1 Combine the raisins, chopped almonds and mixed peel in a small bowl with the kirsch. Cover and leave to marinate for 6 hours or overnight. Drain the fruits, reserving the kirsch.

2 Place the flaked almonds and flour in a food processor, and process until the nuts are very finely ground, then set aside.

3 Place 125 g (4 oz) of the sugar and 900 ml (1½ pints) water in a large saucepan and bring to the boil, stirring, until the sugar has completely dissolved.

4 Peel the pears and place with the peelings in the simmering syrup. Cover with a disc of greaseproof paper and poach gently for 10-15 minutes or until the pears are tender. Drain the pears and discard the peelings. Return the liquid to the pan with the apricot jam and bubble for 30 minutes or until syrupy. Set aside.

5 Cream together the remaining sugar and the butter until light and fluffy. Add the eggs a little at a time, beating well. Fold in the flour and almond mixture, the kirsch and almond essence, if using.

6 Using a teaspoon, scoop out the base of each pear. Combine a spoonful of the creamed mixture with the nuts and fruit and fill the pears. Place in a 900 ml (1½ pint) shallow, ovenproof dish and spoon round the remaining creamed mixture. Brush the pears with a little of the syrupy glaze.

7 Cook at 200°C (400°F) Mark 6 for 55 minutes-1 hour or until the frangipane is golden brown and just firm to the touch. Cover with foil if browning too much.

8 Brush with a little more glaze and serve with plenty of extra-thick cream.

TO FREEZE: Cool, pack and freeze the cooked pudding at the end of step 7.

TO USE: Thaw overnight at cool room temperature. Cover loosely with foil and reheat at 200°C (400°F) Mark 6 for 30-35 minutes or until heated through.

Tarte Tatin

A classic French dessert of caramelised apples on a pastry base, this dish can be frozen in advance and produced with a flourish to complete a meal in style.

Preparation time: 1 hour
Cooking time: 25-30 minutes
Cals per serving: 750
Serves 6

PASTRY	CARAMEL
225 g (8 oz) plain flour	**125 g (4 oz) butter**
150 g (5 oz) butter	**200 g (7 oz) caster sugar**
1.25 ml (¼ tsp) salt	**1.4-1.5 kg (3-3¼ lb) eating apples**
50 g (2 oz) icing sugar	**juice of ½ lemon**
1 egg	**TO SERVE**
vanilla essence	**cream, vanilla custard sauce or ice cream**

1 To make the pastry, sift the flour on to a work surface; make a hollow in the centre and add the butter with the salt. Work butter and salt together using the fingers of one hand until smooth and pliable (do not work in the flour). Add the icing sugar to the butter mixture and mix in the same way. Add the egg and vanilla essence and mix with butter mixture until it resembles scrambled egg. Cut the flour into the butter mixture with a palette knife. Knead lightly until smooth. Wrap and chill for 1 hour or until firm.

2 For the caramel, melt the butter in a 28 cm (11 inch) tarte tatin mould (see Note) and add the sugar. Peel, quarter and core the apples. Pack tightly in the mould, preferably standing on one end, and cook for 20-25 minutes until well caramelised. (Start on a low heat and increase the heat as the apples begin to produce juice.) Turn the apples round two-thirds of the way through cooking time. Add the lemon juice. Allow the apples to cool.

3 Roll the pastry out so that it is 2.5 cm (1 inch) larger all round than the top of the mould or pan. Lay on top of the cooked apples. Prick the pastry with the tip of a sharp knife. Bake at 220°C (425°F) Mark 7 for 25-30 minutes until the pastry is golden brown all over.

4 Leave to cool for 10 minutes. Invert on to a plate. Serve at room temperature with cream, vanilla custard or ice cream.

TO FREEZE: Cool, pack and freeze at the end of step 3.
TO USE: Thaw at cool room temperature for 1-2 hours. Warm in a low oven, loosely covered with foil, for 10-15 minutes. Complete as in step 4.

NOTE: True tarte tatin moulds are very expensive. Either cook the apples in a non-stick frying pan and transfer to a deep, sloping-sided cake tin to bake, or use a shallow flameproof casserole such as Le Creuset.

Crispy Choux with Banana Cream and Mango Purée

Perfect for entertaining, these are easy to prepare and, as a bonus for slimmers, they are low in calories.

Preparation time: 30 minutes
Cooking time: 30 minutes
Cals per serving: 180
Serves 6

25 g (1 oz) butter	**1 large banana, about 150 g (5 oz)**
125 g (4 oz) sifted plain white flour	**150 ml (¼ pint) thick-set, low-fat natural yogurt**
2 eggs, beaten	**30 ml (2 tbsp) low-calorie sweetener**
1 large ripe mango	**icing sugar, to dust**
5 ml (1 tsp) orange flower water	

1 In a small saucepan, melt the butter with 200 ml (7 fl oz) water. Bring to the boil. Immediately the water reaches a vigorous boil remove from the heat. Tip the flour into the hot liquid. Beat with a wooden spoon until the mixture comes together to form a smooth ball in the centre of the pan. Leave to cool for 15 minutes.

2 Add the beaten eggs, a little at a time, beating well after each addition. The mixture will be thick and glossy.

3 Spoon the mixture into 6 rough mounds on a non-stick baking sheet. Cook at 220°C (425°F) Mark 7 for 25-30 minutes or until well risen, golden brown and firm to the touch.

4 Make a horizontal cut through the middle of each bun and open out. Remove most of the doughy centre and return to the oven for 5-7 minutes to crisp and dry out the inside of the choux. If they start to burn, cover with foil. Leave to cool on a wire rack.

5 Meanwhile, peel the skin and remove the stone from the mango. Blend the flesh in a food processor with the orange flower water until very smooth.

6 Mash the banana. Stir in the yogurt and sweetener. Fill each of the choux buns with a spoonful of banana cream and a generous spoonful of mango purée. Serve within an hour, dusted with icing sugar.

TO FREEZE: Pack and freeze at the end of step 4.
TO USE: Unwrap and thaw at cool room temperature for about 1 hour. Warm the buns in a low oven for about 8 minutes to crisp and dry them out after freezing. Leave to cool on a wire rack then complete as above to serve.

Spiced Plum Brulée

Freeze the unused stem ginger pieces for use in cakes, fruit salads and so on.

Preparation time: 40 minutes
Cooking time: 45 minutes
Cals per serving: 520
Serves 8

1 vanilla pod or 5 ml (1 tsp) vanilla essence	**1 orange**
600 ml (1 pint) double cream	**150 ml (¼ pint) syrup from a jar of stem ginger**
6 egg yolks	**150 ml (¼ pint) red wine**
40 g (1½ oz) caster sugar	**4 cloves**
700 g (1½ lb) plums	**5 cm (2 inch) stick cinnamon**
1 lemon	**75 g (3 oz) demerara sugar**

1 Split open the vanilla pod, then place in a saucepan with the cream. Bring slowly to just below the boil. Take off heat, cover and leave for 30 minutes. Lift out the pod, split and scrape out the seeds into the cream .

2 Meanwhile, place the egg yolks in a medium-size bowl with the caster sugar and vanilla essence, if using. Beat with an electric whisk until thick and light in colour. Pour on the cream, stirring. Rinse the saucepan, then return the cream mixture to it.

3 Cook over a gentle heat for about 10 minutes, stirring all the time, until the custard thickens to the consistency of single cream and will just coat the spoon. Watch the froth on the custard – as it begins to thicken, the froth disappears. Do not boil or the custard will curdle.

4 Strain the custard (gently rubbing to ensure all vanilla seeds go through) into a 1.1 litre (2 pint) shallow dish. Pour hand-hot water into a roasting tin to come halfway up the sides of the dish.

5 Bake at 150°C (300°F) Mark 2 for 45 minutes. The custard should have a skin on top and have firmed up slightly. To test, gently shake the dish: if the custard is set,

it should have a slight wobble, but not be at all runny. Cool, cover and chill for several hours.

6 Halve and stone the plums: pare the rind off the lemon and orange. Place the ginger syrup, wine, cloves, cinnamon and rind in a large sauté pan and bring to the boil. Add the plums and bring back to the boil. Simmer gently for 10 minutes or until the plums are just cooked. Drain the plums, reserving the juice. Return the juice, spices and rind to the pan and boil for 10 minutes or until reduced to 150 ml (¼ pint). Strain the juice over the plums.

7 Arrange the plums (cut side down) on top of the custard, then spoon over the syrup. Sprinkle over the demerara sugar and place under the grill for 3-4 minutes or until bubbling. Chill for 30 minutes before serving.

TO FREEZE: At the end of step 6 cool quickly, freeze custard and plums separately.
TO USE: Thaw overnight at cool room temperature and continue as in step 7.

Brioche Summer Puddings

Made with eggs and butter, brioche is richer in flavour than standard bread and gives the finished puddings a wonderful texture. However, if brioche is unavailable, sliced white bread is a perfectly acceptable alternative. Allow very fresh brioche or bread to dry out a little before using.

Preparation time: 30 minutes, plus chilling
Cooking time: 10 minutes
Cals per serving: 250
Serves 8

275 g (10 oz) brioche	**lemon juice, to taste**
450 g (1 lb) redcurrants	**TO SERVE**
700 g (1½ lb) blackberries	**summer berries**
175 g (6 oz) caster sugar	**clotted cream**
30 ml (2 tbsp) Crème de Cassis or blackcurrant cordial	

1 Remove the crusts and cut the brioche into 10-12 slices. Using a 6.5 cm (2½ inch) plain round cutter, cut two circles to form the bases. Halve the remaining brioche slices.

2 Place the circles of brioche in the base of two 1.1 litre (2 pint) fluted charlotte moulds or pudding basins and line the sides with the slices.

3 To make the filling, place the fruit in a large pan with the sugar. Heat gently, for about 5-10 minutes, stirring occasionally, until the fruit releases its juices and the sugar has dissolved. Add the Crème de Cassis or cordial and a little lemon juice to the fruit mixture. Fill the lined moulds.

4 Top with any remaining slices of brioche. Cover with cling film and place on a tray to catch any juices. Weigh down the puddings with tins from the storecupboard and refrigerate overnight.

5 To serve, trim any ragged edges of brioche and carefully unmould the puddings on to deep serving plates. Decorate with summer berries and serve with clotted cream.

TO FREEZE: Cover and freeze at the end of step 4.
TO USE: Thaw overnight in the refrigerator.

Passion Fruit and Mango Soufflé

Surprisingly easy to make, this cold soufflé freezes well and provides an impressive finale
for a dinner party. Serve with delicate sweet biscuits, such as ginger snaps.

Preparation time: 40 minutes, plus chilling
Cooking time: 3 minutes
Cals per serving: 320
Serves 10

three 14 oz (700 g) cans mangoes, drained	**125 g (4 oz) caster sugar**
3 large passion fruit	**300 ml (½ pint) double cream**
50 ml (2 fl oz) fresh orange juice	**TO DECORATE**
30 ml (2 tbsp) powdered gelatine	**star fruit**
4 eggs, separated	**mango slices**

1 Place the mangoes in a large saucepan with the pulp of the passion fruit and the orange juice. Heat gently, stirring continuously, for 3-4 minutes or until pulpy. Purée and rub through a nylon sieve; cool. There should be 450-600 ml (¾-1 pint) purée.

2 In a small bowl, sprinkle the gelatine over 90 ml (6 tbsp) water and leave to soak for 5 minutes.

3 Whisk together the egg yolks and sugar until very thick and pale. Gradually whisk in the fruit purée.

4 Place the bowl of gelatine over a pan of gently simmering water for about 2-3 minutes until the gelatine has completely dissolved. Whisk into the fruit mixture.

5 Whip the cream until it just begins to hold its shape. Fold into the mixture. Whisk the egg whites until stiff but not dry and fold in.

6 Pour the mixture into a 2.3 litre (4 pint) serving dish. Refrigerate for about 5 hours to set.

7 Arrange the mango slices and the star fruit over the surface of the soufflé. Serve immediately.

TO FREEZE: Overwrap and freeze at the end of step 6.
TO USE: Thaw for 24 hours in the refrigerator. Finish as in step 7.

Autumn Almond Pancakes

Any leftover pancakes will freeze well without a filling; interleave with greaseproof paper so you can defrost as many as needed.

Preparation time: 40 minutes, plus standing
Cooking time: 45 minutes
Cals per serving: 275
Serves 8

125 g (4 oz) plain white flour	**20 ml (4 tsp) plain white flour**
1 egg, plus 1 egg yolk	**25 ml (5 tsp) cornflour**
15 ml (1 tbsp) oil	**almond essence**
300 ml (½ pint) milk	**30 ml (2 tbsp) double cream**
FILLING	**oil and butter for greasing**
300 ml (½ pint) milk	**a little melted butter**
75 g (3 oz) ground almonds	**icing sugar for dusting**
2 eggs, separated	**TO SERVE**
50 g (2 oz) caster sugar	**poached plums and blackberries**

1 Blend the flour, egg, egg yolk, oil and milk in a processor until the batter is the thickness of single cream. Cover; set aside in a cool place for at least 30 minutes.

2 Meanwhile, make the filling. Bring the milk and ground almonds slowly to the boil, cover and set aside for 15 minutes. Beat the egg yolks with 25 g (1 oz) sugar until fluffy. Beat in the flours, then blend in the milk mixture. Return to the rinsed-out pan and stir slowly to the boil. Add a few drops of almond essence and float the cream on the top to prevent a skin forming. Cover and cool.

3 Whisk the egg whites until stiff, then whisk in the remaining sugar to make a stiff, shiny mixture; carefully fold into the cooled custard. Cover; set aside.

4 Heat and lightly oil an 18 cm (7 inch) base pancake pan. Fry paper-thin pancakes and set aside.

5 Lightly butter an 18-20.5 cm (7-8 inch) round ovenproof dish. Lay a pancake in the bottom, spread about 30 ml (2 tbsp) custard on the pancake and lay a second pancake on top. Continue until all the filling is used. Finish with a pancake – you will probably use 8 in all. Brush the top with melted butter.

6 Dust heavily with icing sugar and cook at 220°C (425°F) Mark 7 for 40-45 minutes or until hot to the centre. Cover the pancakes with foil if they are becoming too brown. Cut into wedges and serve immediately with poached plums and blackberries.

TO FREEZE: Complete to the end of step 5, wrap and freeze.

TO USE: From frozen, continue as in step 6, covering the pancakes after 30-35 minutes and cooking for 50 minutes more, until hot through.

Panettone Bread and Butter Pudding

Panettone is a dome-shaped yeasted cake with sultanas, orange and citrus peel. Here it is used to turn a family pudding into something special. The cake is found in major supermarkets and delicatessens.

Preparation time: 30 minutes, plus soaking and standing
Cooking time: 1¼ hours
Cals per serving: 705
Serves 8

125 g (4 oz) raisins	**600 ml (1 pint) milk**
100 ml (4 fl oz) brandy	**panettone weighing about 700 g (1½ lb)**
200 g (7 oz) plain chocolate	**75 g (3 oz) softened butter, plus extra for greasing**
two 500 g cartons fresh custard,	**icing sugar for dusting**
about 900 ml (1½ pints) in total	

1 Soak the raisins in the brandy overnight. Roughly chop the chocolate. Stir the custard and milk together.

2 Slice the panettone into circles, about 5 mm (¼ inch) thick, and spread with the butter. Cut into quarters. Grease a 3.4 litre (6 pint) ovenproof dish, and pour a thin layer of the custard over the base of the dish.

3 Layer up the panettone, raisins, chocolate and custard, finishing with a layer of custard. Leave to rest for 1 hour.

4 Place the dish in a roasting tin and pour hot water around the dish to come halfway up the sides. Cook at 180°C (350°F) Mark 4 for 1-1¼ hours or until the custard is set and the top has turned a deep brown. Cover with foil after 40 minutes to prevent the top from burning. Dust lightly with icing sugar to serve.

TO FREEZE: Freeze at end of step 3.
TO USE: Thaw overnight in the refrigerator then complete as above.

Marmalade Pudding

A mouthwatering orange and whisky sauce adds a special touch to these individual puddings.

Preparation time: 20 minutes
Cooking time: 45 minutes
Cals per serving: 550
Serves 8

250 g (9 oz) butter, plus extra for greasing	**250 g (9 oz) caster sugar**
175 g (6 oz) self-raising flour, plus extra for dusting	**3 eggs**
5 large oranges	**45 ml (3 tbsp) whisky**
120 ml (8 tbsp) thin-cut marmalade	

1 Melt a little butter and brush it over the inside of eight 150 ml (¼ pint) metal pudding moulds. Base-line with non-stick baking parchment and dust with a little flour. Finely grate the rind and squeeze the juice from 1 orange. Squeeze the juice from another 2 oranges. Peel the remaining 2 oranges, cut the flesh into segments and set aside. Divide 60 ml (4 tbsp) of the marmalade among each of the moulds.

2 Cream together 175 g (6 oz) butter, 175 g (6 oz) caster sugar and the grated orange rind until light and fluffy. Add the eggs a little at a time, beating well. Fold in the flour, 30 ml (2 tbsp) marmalade and 30 ml (2 tbsp) of the orange juice.

3 Divide the sponge mixture between the pudding moulds, levelling the surfaces. Cut eight pieces of foil and non-stick baking parchment, about 18 cm (7 inches) square. Place each piece of foil on top of a parchment piece and make a pleat to allow for expansion. Brush the centre of the parchment with a little melted butter. Tie securely over the moulds, parchment side down.

4 To make the sauce, melt together the remaining 75 g (3 oz) butter and 75 g (3 oz) caster sugar in a small, heavy-based saucepan. Cook, stirring continuously, over a medium heat for 5 minutes or until a golden caramel. Add the whisky and bubble for 1 minute, then add the remaining orange juice, bring to the boil and bubble gently for 15 minutes or until syrupy. Remove from the heat and stir in the remaining 30 ml (2 tbsp) marmalade and the reserved orange segments. Set aside.

5 Stand the moulds in a roasting tin just large enough to hold them. Pour boiling water around to come halfway up the sides of the moulds. Cover the roasting tin with foil. Bake at 190°C (375°F) Mark 5 for about 40-45 minutes or until firm to the touch.

6 To serve, uncover the puddings and loosen the edges with a round-bladed knife. Turn out on to warm plates and spoon over the warm sauce.

TO FREEZE: Prepare the recipe to the end of step 4. Cool the sauce. Wrap and freeze the puddings and sauce separately.
TO USE: Cook the puddings as in step 5 from frozen for about 50-55 minutes. Thaw the sauce overnight at cool room temperature. Warm over a gentle heat to serve.

Double Chocolate Terrine

Rich and indulgent, this chocolate treat is served with a luscious caramel sauce.

Preparation time: 1 hour, plus chilling
Cooking time: 1 hour 10 minutes
Cals per serving: 940

Serves 6

4 eggs, plus 4 yolks	**cocoa powder for dusting**
250 g (9 oz) caster sugar	**CARAMEL SAUCE**
85 g (3½ oz) cocoa powder	**50 g (2 oz) caster sugar**
65 g (2½ oz) unsalted butter	**150 ml (¼ pint) double cream**
65 g (2½ oz) dark chocolate	**TO SERVE**
300 ml (½ pint) double cream	**single cream**
25 g (1 oz) icing sugar	

1 Line a 23 x 30.5 cm (9 x 12 inch) Swiss roll tin with non-stick baking parchment.

2 Separate 4 eggs. Mix the 4yolks with 25 g (1 oz) caster sugar and 25 g (1 oz) cocoa powder. Whisk the 4 egg whites until stiff, then gradually whisk in 75 g (3 oz) caster sugar until stiff and glossy. Beat a quarter of the meringue into the egg yolk mix. Now gently fold this mixture back into the remaining meringue. Spread over the base of the tin. Bake at 150°C (300°F) Mark 2 for 45-55 minutes or until just firm to touch in the centre. Cool, then cover with a damp cloth.

3 Place the butter, chocolate and remaining cocoa powder in a bowl. Set over gently simmering water and stir until the butter and chocolate are melted. Cool.

4 Whip the cream with the icing sugar until it begins to thicken. Beat 4 egg yolks with the remaining 150 g (5 oz) caster sugar until thick and light in colour, then beat into the cooled chocolate mixture. Slowly whisk in the double cream.

5 Line a 1.1 litre (2 pint) loaf tin with non-stick baking parchment. Cut the cake into 3 rectangles that will fit in the tin. Place one-third of the mousse in the tin and put a piece of cake on top. Repeat until all the mousse and cake are used, finishing with cake. Cover with foil and chill overnight.

6 To make the caramel sauce, melt the sugar slowly in a small heavy-based saucepan until liquid and golden, then cook over a gentle heat until a dark caramel. Add the cream immediately in a slow, steady stream (take care: the hot caramel will cause the cream to boil up in the pan). Stir over a gentle heat until the caramel has melted; cool.

7 Turn out the terrine and thickly slice. Lightly dust with cocoa powder. Serve with chilled single cream and the caramel sauce.

TO FREEZE: Wrap and freeze the completed terrine and sauce separately.
TO USE: Thaw overnight in the refrigerator.

Chocolate and Orange Cheesecake

Cheesecakes are always popular with everyone, especially when flavoured with a winning combination of chocolate and orange. This is a baked type which can be conveniently cooked from frozen.

Preparation time: 35 minutes
Cooking time: 1 hour 10 minutes
Cals per serving: 630-470
Serves 6-8

2 large oranges	**125 g (4 oz) dark chocolate**
3 eggs	**TO DECORATE**
125 g (4 oz) caster sugar	**orange segments**
three 200 g (7 oz) tubs full-fat soft cheese	**chocolate curls**
90 ml (6 tbsp) crème fraîche or thick Greek yogurt	**icing sugar**

1 Grate the rind of the oranges. Line the base of a 23 cm (9 inch) spring-release tin with non-stick baking parchment.

2 Separate the eggs. Beat the egg yolks with 50 g (2 oz) sugar until pale in colour and thick. Add the full-fat soft cheese and crème fraîche or Greek yogurt and beat until smooth.

3 Melt the chocolate in a large bowl over a saucepan of simmering water. Add one-third of the cheese mixture to the chocolate, mix until smooth and put to one side.

4 Add the grated orange rind to the remaining cheese mixture.

5 Whisk the egg whites until stiff and then gradually whisk in the remaining sugar until the mixture is stiff and shiny.

6 Fold one third of the egg whites into the chocolate mixture, spoon into the prepared spring-release tin and smooth the top. Fold the remaining egg whites into the orange mixture, spoon on top of the chocolate mixture and level the top.

7 Bake at 180°C (350°F) Mark 4 for 55-60 minutes or until the centre is just firm to the touch. Turn off the oven and allow the cheesecake to cool in the oven.

8 Unmould the cheesecake. Decorate with orange segments and chocolate curls. Dust with icing sugar.

TO FREEZE: Wrap and freeze at the end of step 6.
TO USE: Bake from frozen at 180°C (350°F) Mark 4 for 1 hour-1 hour 10 minutes, then complete as above.

Iced Lime Mousse

A refreshing mousse that can be served straight from the freezer is a great dessert for entertaining. Try mixing the summer berry decoration with a sauce of puréed sweetened strawberries for a special finishing touch.

Preparation time: 10 minutes, plus freezing
Cooking time: about 20 minutes
Cals per serving: 520
Serves 8

125 g (4 oz) butter	**450 ml (¾ pint) double cream**
5 eggs	**TO SERVE**
200 g (7 oz) caster sugar	**mixed summer berries**
grated rind and juice of 5-6 limes	

1 Place the butter in a bowl and melt over a pan of gently simmering water.

2 Using an electric whisk, beat the eggs and sugar until pale and mousse-like and doubled in volume. Add the butter. Continue whisking over a gentle heat until the mixture thickens and leaves a trail on itself for 2-3 seconds. (This will take about 20 minutes.)

3 Remove from the heat. Stir in the grated lime rind and 175 ml (6 fl oz) lime juice. Cool.

4 Whip the cream until it just holds its shape, then fold into the lime mixture. Pour into a freezerproof serving dish and freeze for at least 6 hours, preferably overnight.

5 Allow mousse to stand at room temperature for 5 minutes before serving with mixed berries. Spoon a few berries over the mousse if wished.

Pistachio Ice Cream

An Italian speciality, this pretty-coloured ice cream is delicious served with amaretti biscuits. Allow the ice cream to soften slightly, so that you can scoop it into attractive looking balls to serve.

Preparation time: 15 minutes, plus freezing
Cooking time: 15 minutes
Cals per serving: 555
Serves 6

125 g (4 oz) blanched pistachio nuts (see Note)	**4 eggs, beaten**
15 ml (1 tbsp) cornflour	**300 ml (½ pint) double cream**
175 g (6 oz) caster sugar	**few drops almond essence**
300 ml (½ pint) milk	**few drops edible green food colouring (optional)**

1 Roughly chop the pistachio nuts. Blend the cornflour and caster sugar in a saucepan with a little of the milk to form a smooth paste. Stir in the remaining milk and bring to the boil, stirring constantly.

2 Pour the mixture on to the eggs, stirring continuously. Return the mixture to the saucepan.

3 Stir the custard mixture over a medium heat for about 5 minutes or until thickened. Allow to cool.

4 Lightly whip the cream and fold into the cooled custard. Add the pistachio nuts, almond essence and food colouring, if using.

5 Pour the mixture into a freezerproof container, cover and freeze for 1-2 hours or until just firm.

6 Remove the ice cream from the freezer and beat thoroughly. Return to the freezer for at least 4 hours. Allow to soften at room temperature for 20 minutes before serving.

NOTE: To blanch pistachios, plunge the shelled nuts into boiling water for a few minutes then remove the skins. The blanched nuts are a lovely, bright green.

Spiced Strawberry Sorbet

Pepper and balsamic vinegar complement strawberries perfectly. This sorbet has a deliciously tangy flavour and is also fat-free and low in calories.

Preparation time: 35 minutes, plus standing and freezing

Cooking time: 5 minutes

Cals per serving: 115

Serves 6

700 g (1½ lb) strawberries	**TO DECORATE**
15 ml (1 tbsp) black peppercorns	**sliced strawberries**
125 g (4 oz) caster sugar	**crushed peppercorns**
30 ml (2 tbsp) balsamic vinegar	

1 Wash and hull the strawberries, then, using a pestle and mortar, coarsely grind the peppercorns. Place the sugar and 150 ml (¼ pint) water in a small saucepan and bring to the boil, stirring until the sugar has dissolved. Stir in the peppercorns, remove the pan from the heat, cover and allow to stand for 1 hour.

2 Strain the syrup through a fine sieve and discard the peppercorns. Place the syrup and strawberries in a food processor or blender and purée until smooth. Push the puréed mixture through the sieve, discarding the seeds and other solids. Stir in the vinegar.

3 Turn the mixture into a shallow, freezerproof container and place in the freezer for about 2 hours or until mushy.

4 Remove from the freezer and beat gently with a fork to break down the ice crystals. Return the container to the freezer for another hour, then remove and beat again.

5 Return the container to the freezer and freeze until firm. Alternatively, churn the mixture in an ice-cream machine until thick and almost frozen.

6 Transfer the sorbet to the refrigerator for about 30 minutes. Serve, decorated with strawberries and crushed peppercorns.

BAKING

Date and Ginger Cake

This deliciously moist and sticky cake is simple to make and is very versatile – serve it with tea, coffee or even as a dessert at the end of a meal.

Preparation time: 20 minutes
Cooking time: about 1 hour
Cals per serving: 210
Makes about 16 slices

125 g (4 oz) stoned dates	2 eggs
50 g (2 oz) stem ginger in syrup	150 g (5 oz) golden syrup
2.5 ml (½ tsp) bicarbonate of soda	150 g (5 oz) black treacle
50 ml (2 fl oz) milk	225 g (8 oz) plain flour
125 g (4 oz) butter	7.5 ml (1½ tsp) ground ginger
125 g (4 oz) light soft brown (muscovado) sugar	salt

1 Grease and line a 23 cm (9 inch) square cake tin with non-stick baking parchment. Roughly chop the dates and stem ginger. Stir the bicarbonate of soda into the milk.

2 Beat together the butter and sugar until pale and light. Slowly add the beaten eggs and then stir in the syrup, treacle, milk, chopped dates and stem ginger.

3 Fold in the sifted flour, ground ginger and a pinch of salt. Pour into the prepared tin and bake at 150°C (300°F) Mark 2 for 1 hour or until a skewer inserted into the cake comes out clean. Leave in the tin for 1 hour. Turn out on to a wire rack.

4 Allow the cake to cool completely, then cut into slices to serve.

TO FREEZE: Pack and freeze the cooled cake.
TO USE: Thaw overnight at cool room temperature.

Teatime Cherry Cake

Made with fresh cherries, this summery cake is quite irresistible! Use a cherry stoner to make light work of pitting the cherries.

Preparation time: 20 minutes
Cooking time: 1½ hours
Cals per slice: 315
Makes about 15 slices

250 g (9 oz) butter, plus extra for greasing	175 g (6 oz) self-raising white flour
about 225 g (8 oz) cherries	**ICING**
250 g (9 oz) caster sugar	50 g (2 oz) cherries
7.5 ml (1½ tsp) vanilla essence	50 g (2 oz) icing sugar
4 eggs	
175 g (6 oz) plain white flour, plus 15 ml (1 tbsp) extra	

1 Grease and base-line a 1.7 litre (3 pint) loaf tin. Halve and pit the 225 g (8 oz) cherries and leave to dry on kitchen paper.

2 Cream 250 g (9 oz) butter and the caster sugar together with the vanilla essence. Add the eggs, one at a time, beating them in well after each addition.

3 Sift 175 g (6 oz) plain white flour with the self-raising flour and gently fold into the mixture. Toss the cut cherries in about 15 ml (1 tbsp) plain flour and fold them carefully into the cake mixture. Spoon into the prepared tin.

4 Bake at 180°C (350°F) Mark 4 for about 1½ hours or until golden and a skewer inserted comes out clean. Cover loosely with foil if necessary. Cool in the tin for about 5 minutes, then turn out on to a wire rack to cool completely.

5 To make the icing, place the cherries in a small saucepan with 150 ml (¼ pint) water and simmer for about 5 minutes or until soft. Drain, then push them through a nylon sieve to produce about 50 ml (2 fl oz) juice. Mix with the icing sugar then drizzle over the cooled cake. Leave to set then cut into thick slices and serve.

TO FREEZE: Pack and freeze at the end of step 4.
TO USE: Thaw at cool room temperature. Complete as in step 5.

Chocolate Mousse Cake

This adaptable, melt-in-the-mouth rich chocolate cake is easy to make and freezes to perfection. It is delicious with a cup of strong black coffee, or cut it into small squares, slip it into petits fours cases and serve it at the end of a meal for a special occasion.

Preparation time: 20 minutes
Cooking time: 1 hour
Cals per serving: 570 - 285
Serves 6 - 12

375 g (13 oz) plain chocolate	**3 eggs**
5 ml (1 tsp) instant coffee granules	**50 g (2 oz) caster sugar**
175 ml (6 fl oz) double cream	**25 g (1 oz) butter**
15 ml (1 tbsp) brandy	

1 Grease and base-line a 16 cm (6½ inch) square base measurement and 4 cm (1½ inch) deep tin with non-stick baking parchment. Break the chocolate into small pieces.

2 To prepare the cake, place 200 g (7 oz) chocolate in a small bowl with the instant coffee. Melt over a pan of simmering water, stirring from time to time. Allow to cool.

3 Whip 100 ml (4 fl oz) double cream until it just holds its shape, then whisk in the brandy. Whisk the eggs and sugar together until pale in colour and thick.

4 Fold the melted chocolate into the egg mixture, followed by the cream, making sure the ingredients are thoroughly mixed. Pour into the prepared tin and place in a roasting tin. Pour in enough hot water to come at least halfway up the sides of the tin. Bake at 180°C (350°F) Mark 4 for 45-60 minutes or until just firm to the centre. Allow to cool in the tin.

5 To make the topping, place the remaining chocolate and cream in a small pan. Melt over a low heat, stirring until melted. Add the butter; stir until melted. Cool, stirring occasionally, until spreadable.

6 Turn the cake out on to a cutting board when cool. Spread the topping evenly over the cake. Chill until just firm. Serve the cake at room temperature, otherwise the topping may be too solid.

TO FREEZE: Wrap and freeze at the end of step 6.
TO USE: Thaw at cool room temperature for 1-2 hours, cut into 6 or 12 rectangles with a sharp knife.

Lemon Seed Cake

This cake is deliciously light and lemony and very low in fat – a treat for those watching their weight.

Preparation time: 20 minutes
Cooking time: 1 hour
Cals per serving: 200
Makes 12 slices

3 lemons	**1 egg**
50 g (2 oz) butter, plus a little extra for greasing	**100 ml (4 fl oz) semi-skimmed milk**
250 g (9 oz) caster sugar	**30 ml (2 tbsp) natural yogurt**
250 g (9 oz) self-raising white flour	**30 ml (2 tbsp) poppy seeds**
5 ml (1 tsp) baking powder	

1 Grate the rind of 1 lemon. Lightly grease and base-line a 900 g (2 lb) loaf tin.

2 Process the butter in a food processor until soft. Add the lemon rind, 200 g (7 oz) sugar, the flour, baking powder, egg, milk, yogurt and poppy seeds. Process until smooth.

3 Turn the mixture into the tin; level the top. Cook at 180°C (350°F) Mark 4 for 55-60 minutes or until cooked through (cover after 40 minutes, if necessary). Cool in the tin for 10 minutes.

4 For the syrup, squeeze the juice from the lemon with rind removed, plus 1 more lemon. Thinly slice the third lemon. Place together in a pan with remaining sugar and 150 ml (¼ pint) water. Bring to the boil and bubble for 4-5 minutes or until syrupy. Remove from the heat.

5 Loosen the sides of the cake with a knife and turn out. Using a cocktail stick, pierce the cake in several places. Spoon the syrup and lemon slices over.

TO FREEZE: Complete to the end of step 3, wrap and freeze.
TO USE: Thaw for 4 hours at cool room temperature. Complete as above.

Sticky Almond Cake

A wonderful teatime treat, this loaf-shaped cake conceals a layer of marzipan through the centre. Try serving the cake sliced, toasted and spread with a little butter.

Preparation time: 30 minutes, plus resting
Cooking time: 1 hour
Cals per serving: 675
Serves 10

200 g (7 oz) butter, plus extra for greasing	**2.5 ml (½ tsp) ground nutmeg**
225 g (8 oz) raisins	**2.5 ml (½ tsp) ground cinnamon**
125 g (4 oz) currants	**3 cardamom pods**
175 g (6 oz) citrus peel	**40 g (1½ oz) ground almonds**
60 ml (4 tbsp) almond-flavoured liqueur, such as Amaretto di Soronno	**20 ml (4 tsp) easy-blend yeast (about 2 sachets)**
150 ml (¼ pint) milk	**grated rind of 1 lemon**
125 g (4 oz) caster sugar	**1 egg, beaten**
450 g (1 lb) strong plain flour	**250 g (9 oz) white marzipan**
2.5 ml (½ tsp) salt	**TO DECORATE**
	icing sugar

1 Lightly grease a large, heatproof bowl and a baking sheet, about 30.5 cm (12 inches) square, with melted butter. Set aside.

2 Place the raisins, currants and citrus peel in a bowl, stir in the Amaretto and set aside.

3 Place 125 g (4 oz) butter, the milk and caster sugar in a small saucepan and warm over a low heat until the butter has melted. Cool until just tepid.

4 Sift the flour, salt, nutmeg and cinnamon into a large bowl. Remove the black seeds from the cardamom pods and crush. Add to the bowl with the ground almonds and yeast. Mix together. Make a well in the centre, add the tepid milk mixture, lemon rind and beaten egg. Stir until evenly mixed. Tip on to a lightly floured surface and knead for about 4 minutes (see Note). Knead the soaked fruit into the dough until just combined.

5 Place in the greased bowl, cover and leave to rise in a warm place for 3 hours. (The dough will not rise dramatically due to the richness and amount of fruit.)

6 Tip the dough on to a lightly floured surface and knead for about 1 minute. Shape into an oval about 30.5 cm (12 inches) long and 20.5 cm (8 inches) wide. Place on the prepared baking sheet.

7 Roll the marzipan into a sausage almost as long as the dough and place in the centre. Lift one of the long sides over to cover the marzipan; repeat with the other side, overlapping in the centre and sealing well at the ends.

8 Flip the roll over so that the sealed ends are underneath and leave in a warm place for 1 hour.

9 Bake at 200°C (400°F) Mark 6 for 15 minutes and then lower the temperature to 180°F (350°F) Mark 4 for 45-55 minutes. Cover loosely with foil if it overbrowns.

10 Melt the remaining butter and brush generously over the hot loaf. Dust heavily with icing sugar. Serve warm or cold.

TO FREEZE: Cool, wrap and freeze at the end of step 9.

TO USE: Thaw overnight at cool room temperature. Wrap in foil and warm through in a low oven for 10-15 minutes. Complete as in step 10.

Note: The mixture will be sticky and almost greasy. If it's very unworkable, add a little more flour.

Pineapple and Coconut Cake

Baked in a loaf tin, this cake has a high fibre content and is relatively low in calories.
A useful cake to have in the freezer.

Preparation time: 20 minutes
Cooking time: 50 minutes
Cals per slice: 250
Makes 10 slices

400 g (14 oz) can pineapple in natural juice	**1.25 ml (¼ tsp) mixed spice**
125 g (4 oz) butter, plus a little extra for greasing	**50 g (2 oz) desiccated coconut**
150 g (5 oz) wholemeal flour	**TO DECORATE**
125 g (4 oz) soft dark brown (muscovado) sugar	**desiccated coconut**
2 eggs	**icing sugar**
10 ml (2 tsp) baking powder	

1 Drain the pineapple well and roughly chop. Grease and base line a 450 g (1 lb) loaf tin.

2 Place the flour and sugar in a food processor and blend for 1-2 minutes or until well mixed. Add the remaining ingredients and mix until smooth.

3 Turn the mixture into the prepared tin, level the surface and brush lightly with 30 ml (2 tbsp) cold water. Cook at 180°C (350°F) Mark 4 for 50 minutes or until cooked (if necessary, cover after 40 minutes).

4 Allow the cake to cool in the tin for 10 minutes, then transfer to a wire rack to cool. Decorate with a little desiccated coconut and icing sugar.

TO FREEZE: Cool, wrap and freeze without decorating at the end of step 4.

TO USE: Thaw for 4 hours at cool room temperature, then decorate.

Chocolate Brownies

Guaranteed to go down well with both family and friends, these delicious squares of moist chocolate and walnut sponge are good served on their own in a lunch-box or for tea, but are equally delicious served as a dessert.

Preparation time: 15 minutes
Cooking time: 30 minutes
Cals per piece: 160
Makes 15 pieces

175 g (6 oz) very low-fat spread	**50 g (2 oz) milk chocolate drops**
125 g (4 oz) soft dark brown sugar	**3 eggs, lightly beaten**
150 g (5 oz) self-raising wholemeal flour	**45 ml (3 tbsp) skimmed milk**
5 ml (1 tsp) baking powder	**TO SERVE**
30 ml (2 tbsp) cocoa powder	**thin custard**
50 g (2 oz) walnut pieces	**chocolate shavings**

1 Lightly grease a 3.5 cm (1½ inch) deep, 27.5 x 17.5 cm (10¾ x 7 inch) tin then line with non-stick baking parchment.

2 Gently heat the low-fat spread and the sugar together until smooth. Cool slightly.

3 Place the flour, baking powder and cocoa powder in a bowl. Stir in the nuts (roughly chopped if large) and the chocolate drops.

4 Make a well in the centre and pour in the cooled sugar mixture and lightly beaten eggs and milk. Beat well until thoroughly mixed. Pour into the prepared cake tin.

5 Bake at 180°C (350°F) Mark 4 for about 30-35 minutes or until just firm to the touch.

6 Allow to cool slightly in the tin, then turn out on to a wire rack to cool completely.

7 To serve, cut into 15 pieces and serve with thin custard and shavings of chocolate.

TO FREEZE: Cool, pack and freeze at the end of step 6.
TO USE: Thaw at cool room temperature for about 3 hours, then serve as in step 7.

Mini Florentines

Served with coffee, these delicate nutty biscuits are perfect for rounding off a reception party. Alternatively, store them in the freezer and use them in smaller batches.

Preparation time: 15 minutes, plus cooling
Cooking time: about 10 minutes
Cals per Florentine (without chocolate): 15
Makes about 74

25 g (1 oz) walnut pieces	**50 g (2 oz) butter, plus extra for greasing**
25 g (1 oz) flaked almonds	**50 g (2 oz) caster sugar**
15 ml (1 tbsp) sultanas	**15 ml (1 tbsp) double cream**
15 ml (1 tbsp) chopped peel	**125 g (4 oz) plain chocolate (optional)**
15 g (½ oz) glacé cherries	

1 Finely chop the nuts, sultanas, peel and cherries and mix together. Grease some baking sheets.

2 Melt the butter in a saucepan, add the sugar and stir over a gentle heat until the sugar dissolves. Bring to the boil and boil for 1 minute. When the mixture turns a light golden colour, take off the heat and stir in the fruit, nuts and cream.

3 Place tiny amounts – no more than 2.5 ml (½ tsp) – on the prepared baking sheets, flattening slightly. Bake at 180°C (350°F) Mark 4 for 5-6 minutes until golden. Leave to cool for 1 minute, then ease off the baking sheet, using a fish slice, and place on a wire rack ɔ cool and harden.

4 If using, melt the chocolate, cool slightly, then brush onto one side of each Florentine. When hard, place in an airtight container, layered with greaseproof paper.

TO FREEZE: Cool, pack and freeze, with or without chocolate.

TO USE: Thaw at cool room temperature for about 2 hours.

Mini Hot Cross Buns

Spicy little fruit buns, traditionally served at Easter time. Once removed from the freezer, they thaw quite quickly and only need to be warmed through to serve.

Preparation time: 30 minutes, plus rising

Cooking time: 18 minutes

Cals per serving: 95

Makes 25

15 g (½ oz) fresh yeast or 7 g (¼ oz) sachet fast-action dried yeast	**50 g (2 oz) butter**
about 175 ml (6 fl oz) tepid milk	**finely grated rind of 1 lemon**
350 g (12 oz) strong pain white flour	**25 g (1 oz) caster sugar**
5 ml (1 tsp) salt	**75 g (3 oz) currants**
5 ml (1 tsp) ground mixed spice	**25 g (1 oz) chopped mixed peel**
5 ml (1 tsp) ground cinnamon	**1 egg, beaten**
5 ml (1 tsp) ground nutmeg	**75 g (3 oz) ready-made shortcrust pastry**
	beaten egg, to glaze

1 If using fresh yeast, blend with the milk. Sift the flour, salt and spices into a bowl and rub in the butter. Stir in the lemon rind, sugar, currants, mixed peel and fast-action dried yeast if using. Make a well in the centre; add yeast liquid or milk and egg. Beat to form a soft dough, adding a little more milk if necessary.

2 Turn out the dough on to a floured surface and, with floured hands, knead for about 8-10 minutes or until the dough is elastic and almost smooth. Place in a large, lightly oiled bowl. Cover with oiled cling film and leave in a warm place until doubled in size; this usually takes 1½-2 hours.

3 Knock down the dough and knead lightly for 1-2 minutes. Divide the dough into about 25 equal-sized pieces and knead each one into a small ball. Place on buttered baking sheets, seam-side down, and flatten slightly with the heel of your hand.

4 Roll out the pastry and cut into narrow strips. Brush the buns with egg to glaze and top each one with a pastry cross. Glaze again. Leave in a warm place until doubled in size; about 30 minutes.

5 Bake at 190°C (375°F) Mark 5 for 15-18 minutes until they sound hollow when tapped. Cool on wire racks.

TO FREEZE: Pack and freeze at the end of step 5.

TO USE: Thaw for about 3 hours, then warm through to serve.

Savoury Saffron Muffins

Serve these savoury muffins warm as part of an al fresco spread. Half the muffins
are flavoured with spinach and feta, while the other half are made with sun-dried tomatoes,
olives and mozzarella.

Preparation time: 30 minutes
Cooking time: 20 minutes
Cals per muffin: 130
Makes 12

50 g (2 oz) butter, melted	**SPINACH AND FETA FLAVOURING**
250 g (9 oz) plain white flour	**225 g (8 oz) spinach**
25 g (1 oz) baking powder	**50 g (2 oz) feta cheese**
5 ml (1 tsp) salt	**15 ml (1 tbsp) chopped fresh thyme**
2 eggs	**pepper**
200 ml (7 fl oz) milk	**ITALIAN FLAVOURING**
pinch of saffron strands	**25 g (1 oz) sun-dried tomatoes**
	25 g (1 oz) black and green pitted olives
	125 g (4 oz) mozzarella cheese

1 To make the spinach and feta flavouring, cook the spinach, then drain and chop finely. Chop the feta cheese and mix with the spinach. Add the thyme and season with salt and pepper. Beat until smooth.

2 To make the Italian flavouring, finely chop the sun-dried tomatoes, olives and mozzarella cheese. Mix together.

3 Brush 12 large, non-stick muffin tins with 10 ml (2 tsp) melted butter. Sift the flour, baking powder and salt into a mixing bowl. Beat in the eggs, milk, remaining butter and saffron. Divide mixture between two bowls.

4 Fold a prepared flavouring into each bowl. Spoon the mixtures into the muffin tins.

5 Cook at 200°C (400°F) Mark 6 for 15-20 minutes until golden brown and well risen.

TO FREEZE: Cool, pack and freeze the baked muffins.
TO USE: Thaw at room temperature for about 2 hours.
Warm through in a hot oven for 5 minutes before serving.

Apple and Cheese Bread

A lovely savoury bread, with a tang of apples and cheese. Perfect to serve as part of a cold spread with cheese and cold meat or as an accompaniment to a vegetable soup.

Preparation time: 10 minutes
Cooking time: 1 hour
Cals per slice: 210
Serves 4

25 g (1 oz) butter	**125 g (4 oz) mature Cheddar cheese**
225 g (8 oz) self-raising white flour	**salt and pepper**
10 ml (2 tsp) baking powder	**1 egg, lightly beaten**
10 ml (2 tsp) mustard powder	**15 ml (1 tbsp) porridge oats**
2 crisp apples	

1 Rub the butter into the flour, baking powder and mustard powder. Coarsely grate the apples and cheese and stir into the rubbed-in mixture. Season with salt and pepper and bind with the egg, reserving 5 ml (1 tsp) egg.

2 On a lightly floured surface, shape the dough into an 18 cm (7 inch) round and place on a greased baking sheet. Slash the top, brush with the reserved egg and sprinkle the oats over.

3 Bake at 190°C (350°F) Mark 5 for 50 minutes, then turn and cook for 10 minutes. Cool on a wire rack. Serve warm or cold.

TO FREEZE: Cool, pack and freeze at end of step 3.
TO USE: Thaw overnight at cool room temperature; refresh in a warm oven for 15 minutes.

Olive and Walnut Bread

Flavoured with black olives, tangy walnuts and fresh parsley, this delicious bread should be served warm and thickly sliced. A stylish addition to any meal.

Preparation time: 25 minutes, plus rising

Cooking time: 37 minutes

Cals per slice: 125

Makes two loaves (12 slices each)

125 g (4 oz) pitted black olives	**7 g (¼ oz) sachet fast-action dried yeast**
75 g (3 oz) walnuts	**75 ml (5 tbsp) chopped fresh parsley**
600 g (1 lb 5 oz) strong plain white flour	**olive oil**
10 ml (2 tsp) salt	

1 Roughly chop the olives; finely chop the walnuts. Mix both together with the flour, salt, yeast and parsley.

2 Make a well in the centre of the dry ingredients and add 375 ml (13 fl oz) tepid water mixed with 45 ml (3 tbsp) oil. Stir together to form a soft dough, adding a little more water if necessary.

3 Turn the dough onto a well-floured surface and knead well for about 10 minutes until it is smooth and elastic.

4 Divide the dough in half and shape each piece into a roll 18-20.5 cm (7-8 inches) long. Place the rolls of dough on separate oiled baking sheets and cover loosely with lightly oiled cling film.

5 Leave the dough in a warm place for 30-40 minutes or until doubled in size. Lightly slash the tops.

6 Bake at 220°C (425°F) Mark 7 for 12 minutes. Lower the temperature to 180°C (350°F) Mark 4 for a further 25 minutes or until well browned and sounding hollow when tapped. Leave to cool for a few minutes on wire racks. Serve warm.

TO FREEZE: Cool, wrap and freeze at the end of step 6.
TO USE: Thaw overnight at cool room temperature. Reheat at 200°C (400°F) Mark 6 for 15-20 minutes, wrapped in foil.

Wholemeal Bread

It's always useful to have a loaf of bread in the freezer – this bread is a good all-rounder and can be shaped into batons if preferred.

Preparation time: 25 minutes, plus rising
Cooking time: about 35 minutes
Cals per slice: 140
Makes one loaf (12 slices)

450 g (1 lb) plain wholemeal flour	**25 g (1 oz) butter or margarine**
5 ml (1 tsp) salt	**150 ml (¼ pint) tepid milk**
5 ml (1 tsp) caster sugar	**oil for greasing**
7 g (¼ oz) sachet fast-action dried yeast	

1 Mix the flour, salt and sugar in a bowl, and stir in the dried yeast. Rub in the butter. Make a well in the centre; pour in the milk and about 175 ml (6 fl oz) tepid water. Mix to a soft dough.

2 Turn out the dough on to a lightly floured surface and knead for about 10 minutes until smooth and elastic.

3 Lightly grease a 900 g (2 lb) loaf tin. Flatten the dough to an oblong the length of the loaf tin but three times as wide. Fold the bottom third up over the centre and the top third down. Press down well. Turn over, then place in the tin.

4 Cover the dough with oiled cling film and leave in a warm place for about 45 minutes until risen.

5 Brush the top with water and bake at 220°C (425°F) Mark 7 for 20 minutes. Reduce the temperature to 180°C (350°F) Mark 4 and remove bread from tin. Bake for a further 15 minutes. To test, tap the bottom crust; the bread should sound hollow. Cool on a wire rack.

TO FREEZE: Wrap and freeze at the end of step 5.
TO USE: Thaw overnight at cool room temperature.

NOTE: For batons, divide the dough in half and shape each piece into a long roll with tapering ends, about 35 cm (14 inches) long. Place on a greased baking sheet.

SAUCES AND BUTTERS

Chicken Stock

There are many ready-made stocks available in the shops, but they tend to be rather salty and their flavour does not compare to home-made stock, which is very easy to make and can be frozen for future use.

Preparation time: 10 minutes
Cooking time: 3-4 hours
Makes about 1.1 litres (2 pints)

2 onions	**small bunch each parsley and thyme**
1 carrot	**2 bay leaves**
2 celery sticks	**10 peppercorns**
chicken bones, about 900 g-1.4 kg (2-3 lb)	**salt and pepper**

1 Peel and slice the onions and carrot; slice the celery. Place the onions, carrot and celery in a large saucepan with the bones. Cover with about 2.8 litres (5 pints) cold water. Bring slowly to the boil. Skim the top and add the parsley, thyme, bay leaves and peppercorns.

2 Simmer very gently for 3-4 hours, skimming frequently. The liquid should reduce to half the original quantity.

3 Strain and reserve the liquid, cool quickly and refrigerate. Skim any fat from the stock once it has chilled. Season with salt and pepper to taste.

TO FREEZE: Cool, pack and freeze at the end of the recipe.
TO USE: Thaw overnight at cool room temperature.

VARIATION
Vegetable Stock: To make 750 ml (1¼ pints) vegetable stock, place the onions in a large saucepan with 3 chopped carrots, 4 chopped celery sticks and 1.1 litres (2 pints) water. Bring slowly to the boil, skimming off any impurities, then add the parsley, thyme, bay leaves and peppercorns. Simmer for 30 minutes then strain reserving the liquid. Season and cool.

Béchamel Sauce

A classic white sauce – just add grated cheese, chopped parsley or sautéed onion to create different sauces to serve with meat, fish and vegetables.

Preparation time: 5 minutes, plus standing
Cooking time: 5 minutes
Cals per 150 ml (¼ pint): 180
Makes 300 ml (½ pint)

300 ml (½ pint) milk	**15 g (½ oz) butter or margarine**
1 slice of onion	**15 g (½ oz) plain white flour**
1 bay leaf	**salt and pepper**
6 peppercorns	**freshly grated nutmeg**
1 blade of mace	

1 Pour the milk into a saucepan. Add the onion, bay leaf, peppercorns and mace. Bring to scalding point, remove from heat, cover and infuse for 10-30 minutes. Strain.

2 To make the roux, melt the butter in a saucepan. Stir in the flour and cook, stirring, for 1 minute.

3 Remove from the heat and gradually pour on the warm milk, whisking constantly. Season lightly with salt, pepper and nutmeg.

4 Return to the heat and bring to the boil, whisking constantly until the sauce thickens and is smooth. Simmer for 2-3 minutes.

TO FREEZE: Cool, pack and freeze at the end of step 4.
TO USE: Thaw overnight at cool room temperature, then reheat.

VARIATIONS

Cheese Sauce: Off the heat, stir in 50 g (2 oz) finely grated mature Cheddar or Gruyère cheese and a large pinch of mustard powder.

Parsley Sauce: Add about 30 ml (2 tbsp) chopped parsley.

Onion Sauce: Finely dice 1 onion, then sauté in a little butter for 10-15 minutes until softened. Stir into the Bechamél. Purée in a blender or food processor, if preferred.

Fresh Tomato Sauce

In summer, when tomatoes are plentiful, make up batches of this sauce and freeze for use in the winter months.

Preparation time: 10 minutes
Cooking time: 1 hour
Cals per serving: 105
Serves 4

900 g (2 lb) ripe tomatoes	**5 ml (1 tsp) dried oregano**
2 garlic cloves	**30 ml (2 tbsp) chopped fresh basil**
30 ml (2 tbsp) extra-virgin olive oil	**salt and pepper**
grated rind of 1 lemon	**pinch of sugar (optional)**

1 Roughly chop the tomatoes and peel and crush the garlic. Put the tomatoes, oil, garlic, lemon rind and oregano in a saucepan. Bring to the boil, cover and simmer for 30 minutes.

2 Add the basil, salt and pepper to taste and sugar, if required. Simmer, uncovered for a further 20-30 minutes until the sauce is thickened. If a smooth sauce is preferred, pass through a sieve.

Rich Tomato Sauce

A rich-tasting tomato sauce, perfect for topping pasta or for serving with plainly grilled meat.

Preparation time: 10 minutes
Cooking time: 25-30 minutes
Cals per serving: 175-115
Serves 4-6

1 onion	**45 ml (3 tbsp) sun-dried tomato paste**
2 garlic cloves	**2 oregano sprigs**
two 400 g (14 oz) cans plum tomatoes	**salt and pepper**
50 g (2 oz) butter	

1 Peel and finely chop the onion and garlic. Chop the tomatoes roughly.

2 Melt the butter in a saucepan, add the onion and garlic and cook gently for 5 minutes until softened. Add the tomatoes, sun-dried tomato paste and oregano. Cook, uncovered, over a low heat for 25-30 minutes, stirring occasionally until thick and pulpy. Discard the oregano and season with salt and pepper. Serve at once.

TO FREEZE: Cool, pack and freeze at the end of step 2.

TO USE: Thaw overnight at cool room temperature, then reheat gently.

Cranberry and Orange Sauce

Cranberries are a traditional accompaniment to roast turkey – here they are poached in wine and orange juice to make a tangy, fruit sauce. Freeze the sauce ahead of time to have ready for the celebration or festive turkey.

Preparation time: 10 minutes
Cooking time: 30 minutes
Cals per serving: 110
Serves 8

1 orange	**150 ml (¼ pint) red wine**
350 g (12 oz) fresh or frozen cranberries	**150 ml (¼ pint) orange juice**
175 g (6 oz) caster sugar	

1 Finely grate the orange rind and squeeze the juice. Set the rind aside. Place the cranberries, sugar, wine and both orange juices in a saucepan and bring to the boil. Simmer, uncovered, stirring occasionally, for 30 minutes.

2 Remove and reserve half the cranberries. Blend the remainder of the sauce until smooth. Mix with the reserved cranberries and orange rind. Cool, cover and chill. Serve cold.

TO FREEZE: Pack and freeze at the end of step 2.

TO USE: Thaw overnight at cool room temperature.

Bread Sauce

The classic accompaniment to roast poultry, this version is particularly creamy with a strong hint of cloves, peppercorns and nutmeg. Freeze ahead to simplify preparations for a roast meal.

Preparation time: 5 minutes, plus standing
Cooking time: about 7 minutes
Cals per serving: 355
Serves 8

2 onions	**175 g (6 oz) fresh white breadcrumbs**
6 whole cloves	**300 ml (½ pint) single cream**
600 ml (1 pint) milk	**125 g (4 oz) butter**
4 bay leaves	**10 ml (2 tsp) freshly grated nutmeg**
salt and pepper	**60 ml (4 tbsp) crème fraîche**
6 black peppercorns	

1 Peel the onions, leaving them whole. Stud the whole onions with the cloves. Place them in a saucepan with the milk, bay leaves, seasoning and peppercorns.

2 Bring to the boil, then remove from the heat. Pour into a bowl, cover and set aside for 3 hours.

3 Strain the milk into a saucepan. Over a low heat, gradually add the breadcrumbs. Bring to the boil, stirring. Simmer for 5 minutes or until the sauce thickens. Set aside until required.

4 Gently reheat sauce with the cream, butter, nutmeg and plenty of seasoning. Stir in the crème fraîche just before serving.

TO FREEZE: Cool, pack and freeze at the end of step 3.
TO USE: Thaw overnight at cool room temperature. Reheat and complete step 4.

Mediterranean Relish

Serve this rich-tasting relish with vegetable crudités as a delicious starter. Alternatively use sparingly on pizza bases and top with tomatoes and grated cheese, or toss the relish in hot pasta with lots of grated Parmesan for a quick snack.

Preparation time: 15 minutes, plus marinating and chilling

Cooking time: none

Cals per serving: 235

Serves 6

2 garlic cloves	**10 ml (2 tsp) Dijon mustard**
125 g (4 oz) pitted black olives	**2 egg yolks**
100 ml (4 fl oz) olive oil	**10 ml (2 tsp) lemon juice**
50 g (2 oz) can anchovy fillets	**salt and pepper**
50 g (2 oz) sun-dried tomatoes in oil, drained	

1 Peel and slice the garlic. Place the olives in a bowl with the olive oil and sliced garlic. Cover and leave in a cool place to steep for several hours.

2 Drain the anchovy fillets, place in a bowl, pour over a little cold water and soak for about 20 minutes. Drain the anchovies well.

3 Drain the oil from the olives and reserve. Blend the olives, garlic, anchovies, sun-dried tomatoes and mustard in a food processor until roughly chopped.

4 Add the egg yolks and blend for a few seconds only, then gradually blend in the reserved oil. Lastly, add the lemon juice and seasoning. Spoon into a dish, cover with cling-film and chill for at least 2 hours, preferably overnight.

TO FREEZE: Pack and freeze the completed relish.
TO USE: Thaw at cool room temperature for about 6 hours. Stir well and chill again before serving.

Sabayon Sauce

Delicious with cold fruit desserts, but also an excellent accompaniment to Christmas Pudding. Precise sizes have been given for the pan, bowl and boiling time to ensure the syrup reaches the correct temperature before adding to the egg yolks.

Preparation time: 15 minutes
Cooking time: about 10 minutes
Cals per serving: 115
Serves 8

75 g (3 oz) caster sugar	**100 ml (4 fl oz) double cream**
3 egg yolks	**grated rind and juice of 1 lemon**

1 Place the sugar and 100 ml (4 fl oz) water in a small saucepan, 15 cm (6 inches) in diameter. Dissolve the sugar slowly over a low heat. Increase the heat to high and boil for 7-8 minutes. The liquid should look very syrupy with large pea-size bubbles.

2 Place the egg yolks in a small bowl, 12.5-15 cm (5-6 inches) in diameter. With an electric whisk, beat the yolks together, pour on the hot syrup in a thin stream and whisk until thick, mousse-like and cool.

3 Whip the cream to stiff peaks, add the lemon rind and juice and whip again to soft peaks.

4 Fold the cream into the mousse. Cover and chill overnight.

5 Whisk the sauce well before serving, then transfer to a serving bowl and serve at once.

TO FREEZE: Pack and freeze at the end of step 4.
TO USE: Thaw overnight in the refrigerator.

Apple Sauce

Excellent with roast pork, this apple sauce is also delicious served with fresh blackberries and crème fraîche, or use with lightly whipped cream as a filling for sponge cake.

Preparation time: 10 minutes
Cooking time: 10 minutes
Cals per 25 ml (1 fl oz): 30
Makes 225 ml (8 fl oz)

450 g (1 lb) Bramley apples	**15 g (½ oz) butter**
15 ml (1 tbsp) lemon juice	**caster sugar (optional)**

1 Peel and roughly chop the apples. Place in a saucepan with the lemon juice and 45 ml (3 tbsp) water, cover and simmer for about 10 minutes or until softened.

2 Push through a nylon sieve. Stir in the butter and sweeten to taste, if wished.

TO FREEZE: Cool, pack and freeze.

TO USE: Thaw overnight at cool room temperature.

Herb Butter

Make single-herb butters, such as dill for grilled fish or parsley for cooked peas. Try adding crushed garlic, grated lemon rind or finely chopped chilli, too. Mixed-herb butters are also useful for hot breads, sauces and steaks.

Preparation time: 10 minutes
Cooking time: none
Cals per serving: 215
Serves 6

175 g (6 oz) butter, softened	**60 ml (4 tbsp) chopped fresh herbs**

1 Beat together the butter and herbs. Spoon on to a sheet of greaseproof paper and shape into a rough, thin log.

2 Roll up in the greaseproof paper and chill for about 2 hours until firm.

TO FREEZE: Thickly slice at the end of step 2. Open freeze the slices then pack into polythene bags.

TO USE: Use straight from frozen.

Sun-dried Tomato Butter

Use to top barbecued chicken, steaks and vegetables. Also delicious with baked potatoes, or for tossing with boiled new potatoes.

Preparation time: 10 minutes
Cooking time: none
Cals per serving: 300
Serves 6

1 garlic clove

1 small bunch chives

25 g (1 oz) pitted black olives

25 g (1 oz) sun-dried tomatoes or 30 ml (2 tbsp) sun-dried tomato paste

225 g (8 oz) unsalted butter, softened

pepper

1 Peel the garlic and blend with all ingredients in a food processor until smooth.

2 Roll up in greaseproof paper and chill for about 2 hours or until required.

TO FREEZE: Freeze butter at the end of step 2.

TO USE: Thaw overnight in the refrigerator.

Ginger Butter

Delicious for adding an exotic flavour to vegetables, or try spreading under the skin of a chicken before roasting.

Preparation time: 5 minutes
Cooking time: none
Cals per serving: 155
Serves 6

5 cm (2 inch) piece fresh root ginger

125 g (4 oz) butter, softened

salt and pepper

1 Peel and finely grate the ginger. Beat together with the butter and season well with salt and pepper. Roll up in greaseproof paper and chill for about 2 hours or until required.

TO FREEZE: Wrap and freeze the butter.

TO USE: Thaw overnight at cool room temperature.

Index

INDEX